BETWEEN THE LINES

THE SPIRIT OF
SOUTH AFRICAN RUGBY

BETWEEN THE LINES

THE SPIRIT OF
SOUTH AFRICAN RUGBY

MATTHEW KNIGHT

PENGUIN BOOKS

PENGUIN BOOKS

Published by the Penguin Group
Penguin Books (South Africa) (Pty) Ltd, 24 Sturdee Avenue, Rosebank, Johannesburg 2196, South Africa
Penguin Books Ltd, 80 Strand, London WC2R 0RL, England
Penguin Group (USA) Inc, 375 Hudson Street, New York, New York 10014, USA
Penguin Group (Canada), 90 Eglinton Avenue East, Suite 700, Toronto, Ontario, M4P 2Y3, Canada (a division of Pearson Penguin Canada Inc.)
Penguin Ireland, 25 St Stephen's Green, Dublin 2, Ireland (a division of Penguin Books Ltd)
Penguin Group (Australia), 250 Camberwell Road, Camberwell, Victoria 3124, Australia (a division of Pearson Australia Group Pty Ltd)
Penguin Books India Pvt Ltd, 11 Community Centre, Panchsheel Park, New Delhi – 110 017, India
Penguin Group (NZ), 67 Apollo Drive, Mairangi Bay, Auckland 1310, New Zealand (a division of Pearson New Zealand Ltd)

Penguin Books (South Africa) (Pty) Ltd, Registered Offices:
24 Sturdee Avenue, Rosebank, Johannesburg 2196, South Africa

www.penguinbooks.co.za

First published by Penguin Books (South Africa) (Pty) Ltd 2009

ISBN 9780143026006

Typeset by Nix Design in 11.2/16 pt BruceOldStyle
Cover design: mrdesign
Printed and bound by Ultra Litho, Johannesburg

ACKNOWLEDGMENTS

My parents, Billy and Ruth, for wisely budgeting for my education, even if some of it was to be spent in the boarding house. The Solomons, Derek and Leslee, for fruit salads and green men during those last days of writer's block, and their son Brett, for inspirational 'soul'. The boys and staff of Bickley Park School for support and encouragement – even after the Lions series.

There have been numerous men and women who have passionately contributed their stories. Without them, it would be a rather lean book befitting a wobbly table with one short leg. Particular thanks go to: Nico du Plessis; Ruan van der Merwe; Gerrie Swart and those memorable tickets; Richard Mayer; Ian Pringle; Julian Pienaar; Jono Dickson; Professor John Kannemeyer; Chuma Mbambisa; Chris Taylor; James Thorpe; Desmond Sonnenfeld; Johann Reinecke; Deidre Hickman; Bill Schroder; Andrew Caldwell; EK Moorcroft; Keith Hodgskiss; Chris Bush; Adam Robinson of Lemonwood Cottages; George and Hannetjie Miles; Norman Elwell; and Duncan Buchanan. Endless pages could list the old boys across this land and indeed the world who have submitted treasured thoughts. Thank you all, and I do hope I have done your alma mater justice. The research and anecdotes are also indebted to the numerous administrative staff, coaches and teachers who have given of their time to help me. Thanks also go to the translators who corrected my soutie shortcomings, Tobie Meyer and Chris Brink; and to the folk I've met, interviewed and who have enthused past nostalgia and put thoughts to paper. You have been a driving inspiration for this project. Thanks to artist Tony Grogan and the many who have assisted the history and research: Chris Maxwell; Gerhard Burger; Wim van der Berg and especially Paul Dobson, rugby's Google and always a sagacious sounding board; as well as Trevor Skead and Alex Latimer, great friends who have always offered wise council and unnecessary sarcasm. Thanks to the professional team at Penguin: David Schröder; Louise Grantham and Reneé Naudé. But suffice to say all fallacies and errors in this book are mine to bear alone.

Many thanks to Greg James and the JAG Foundation for their assistance during the book's production, and indeed for their tireless development of rugby and sport at South Africa's grass roots.

Finally and most gratefully to my wife, Kirstin, whose steadfast faith and patience never once told me to act my age.

For Kirstin

FOREWORD

The first time I met Matt Knight was shortly before leaving for the World Cup in France. He had arranged school rugby jerseys from each of the players' old schools for a photo shoot at The Cullinan Hotel. For half an hour old rivalries were again remembered, old scores and big tackles revisited, and the deep fondness each member held for his old school was palpable. Watching Schalk eagerly throw on a striped Paarl Gim jersey and a beaming Bryan don his crimson KES jersey showed me that the roots of their current success lay in the values and ethos they had been exposed to from the very first day at their alma maters.

Rugby is a game where the players are tested – intellectually, physically and emotionally. At the great schools scattered around our country this game is learnt and played in the context of an educational package. It is part of what will mould the young men involved into mature young adults. But it will also establish lasting friendships, something which has always been at the very heart of the game – it is in these early years that the most memorable stories are made, told and retold. Personally, I still hold a deep affinity with schools rugby and remain involved in coaching schools throughout southern Africa. I was also fortunate enough to grow up in a school environment that taught me the values of the game and showed me how it should be played. My own journey would take me full circle – I ended up coaching at Jeppe – and it is because of this that I can confidently boast that South Africa has the healthiest reserves of young, raw talent anywhere in the world. The success of the Springboks is directly related to this. However, these foundations need protection, and it is to Knight's credit that he has travelled these lands to show that at the centre of our healthy grassroots rugby are passionate rugby people who continue to take the game forward. Between these lines, you'll find an author with an eye for this unique game's strange intricacies and traditions and an unreserved love of the characters that have made it what it is in South Africa today.

Jake White

HOW RUGBY WAS MEANT TO BE PLAYED

Bishops

April 2008

GENESIS

Rugby history was made one wintry morning in Durban. Two old rivals had been squaring off against one another from some unreasonable hour of the morning, and the final act of the game was unfolding. The mighty maroon-jerseyed u10Cs were leading their green-clad opponents 12-3, but in a belated burst of enthusiasm the Greens breached the Maroon defence and scored a try beneath the wonky wooden uprights. The Maroon coach, a geography teacher, made the relevant calculations and concluded that his side were safe. He breathed a sigh of relief – the results in Monday's school assembly would please the boys and the boss – as he watched the small Green halfback place the muddied oval ball on a mound of earth with painstaking precision and step back to admire the poles. But then, as the halfback began his oft-practised approach to the ball, it toppled over. For a moment there was confusion. Then anarchy. And, finally, 15 Maroon jerseys charged at the kicker. Petrified, he instinctively scooped up the ball and made haste for the safety of the Maroon corner flag. Flinging himself over the white chalk, he planted the ball without a hand being laid upon him and the young referee, who, it should be said, had thoroughly enjoyed his previous evening unto the early hours, promptly awarded the try.

There were vehement protests from the Maroon side who,

though young of mind, felt that a 10-point try was impossible. But the score stood and the game ended 13-12 in favour of the Greens.[1]

This is kaalvoet rugby; that naive, barefoot version of rugger played over duiwel thorns and upon frozen Saturday morning fields. It rewards the carefree young souls who play it with numb hands, feet and brains, but still they come back for more – even when they've grown older and greyer and don't bounce as well as they did in their youth. What is the attraction to this reckless sport? Some would argue, perhaps, that it is the fact that for most of us it was ingrained as compulsory enjoyment during our school years – where we were forced to sing cheesy school songs and religiously attend First XV games. But for others those blissful days really did offer the true spirit of 'the hooligan's game' and afterwards the strange sport of rugger became a fundamental part of their lives. Whatever the case, its purity and spirit is most tangible in those kaalvoet years.

There are enough rugby stories to fill the shelves of many a musty school library, but in this book I've chosen a few persons – from the old and new school, and every other school for that matter – that I feel encapsulate the spirit of South African rugby. The people you will meet may be largely unfamiliar to you but their impact upon the game has been immense. Their stories, and a few other nostalgic anecdotes I've dragged out, will be enjoyable for any true rugby soul, but particularly those who suffered through those seemingly eternal double science lessons on a Friday afternoon and somehow managed to survive for the big derby that followed.

This book is distinctly South African – that means indigenous words like braai, poppie and soutie will be imperative to either

---

[1] The game, according to Glenwood archivist Kevin Jordan, took place in the mid-1970s and the schools concerned were Kearsney and Glenwood. This was in the days of four-point tries, and though the details around the specific age group and the confused coach remain rather fuzzy, the story is true.

know or learn – and in it I hope to have captured something of the typically tumultuous years of Springbok rugby between World Cup glory in 2007 and the Lions series of 2009. But though 15 Springboks may determine national spirit, by themselves they are just a small piece of the puzzle that is South African rugby. To get to the heart of the game we need to return to our grassroots, to school blazers and ties, war cries and the monotony of a detention.

Let's begin where all good books begin: Genesis. It's been said that only an Englishman could invent a game with an oval ball made from a pig's bladder. It has also been wisely said that 'In 1823 William Webb Ellis first picked up the ball in his arms and ran with it. And for the next 156 years, forwards have been trying to work out why.'[2]

Apparently, we have a lot to thank young Bill for. He broke the forbidden rules with all the demented splendour of a flying winger (a man after my own heart) and in daring to be different created the foundations for the game we know and love today.[3]

However, the strange game didn't spread as quickly as you might think, and by 1861, almost 40 years after Webb Ellis had picked up the ball and run, rugby football was only played at England's Rugby School. Other schools had their own games, which were often adapted to the land available (Eton, for instance, had two games – the wall game and the field game). And although some of the games had similarities to the Rugby game

---

[2] Sir Tasker Watkins (former President of the Welsh Rugby Union).

[3] Historians seem to be unanimous that the school did allow handling at the time, and that the rules he broke were simply his own school rules. Strange also that although William Webb Ellis has become a legendary figure (courtesy of *Tom Brown's Schooldays*), he never, during his lifetime, and in the midst of the game's growth and development, claimed the status now attached to him. There is perhaps then good reason to consider that Ellis only bears the Union baton because Rugby League was growing steadily in the north of England – the Unionists, to add history and prestige to their version of the game and therefore undermine the 'professional' version, gave Webb Ellis status.

– Winchester College had its own game (the Winchester game) in which players also took the ball forward to the opponents' goal and not back home as in ancient games – they had no set form. Those who played the game decided the rules or laws before each match they played.

This, though, was the time when many new public schools sprang up across Britain and began to use the rough game to tame the spirits of their exuberant pupils, and develop them into leaders – muscular Christians who could govern a flourishing empire.[4]

Slowly, the game grew. Clubs fought and argued, but eventually it began to evolve into the game we know today as Rugby Union. Some changes have been a sure improvement on the game. Like the 'try'. A try guaranteed a side no points back in the day, only the opportunity to 'try' to convert your touchdown. In the 1880s Yorkshire outscored Middlesex 4 tries to 0, but they failed to convert a single try and the scoreboard remained unaffected. A solitary drop goal by Middlesex was enough to secure them a 'convincing' 3-0 win.[5] Another change was to the number of players allowed on the pitch. At one stage teams fielded 20 players per team. These days they are limited to 15, and Rugby League – that sacrilegious sport mentioned only in hushed tones followed by 10 Hail Marys – only manages 13.[6] Many other laws have continued to evolve over the years. This was particularly

---

[4] Riots were far from uncommon as the sons of wealthy men rebelled against their poor accommodation and food, and against the impoverished, lower class men employed as teachers. In Winchester, at one stage, the militia was brought in to combat the armed school boys and a classroom was blown up at Rugby School.

[5] Until 1948 the drop goal remained the most valuable single score in the game.

[6] Rugby League came about in the late nineteenth century when it dawned on some smart-arses in the north of England that they deserved to get payment for their weekend bruises (as compensation for their loss of hourly pay). It amounted to grown men being paid to be play rugby; a disgraceful thing for a loyal Unionist. Today, however, it is accepted and encouraged.

so in the late 1980s with the arrival of one Sean Fitzpatrick, who with seemingly good intention repeatedly pointed out many 'overlooked indiscretions' to the ref. This first confused and then infuriated his unwitting opponents.

As Rugby Union began settling on chapter and verse, so specialist positions began to emerge. The naming of positions comes from various sources. It started among the *backs*. There was always one all the way back – the fullback. Then there were two players between the forwards and the fullbacks – the halfway backs, the halfbacks. Then there were three players who were a quarter-way back, the quarterbacks, the three quarters, which produced a semantic problem when a fourth was added.[7] The forwards, bless their simple souls, got ordinary names. They were after all the real men of rugby, the men going forward.

As a teacher, I've had some experience in coaching and siphoning out positions for school boys at an early school age. Players largely remain in these positions for most of their school career. Thus, trials and process of selection is critical, and in some cases may determine whether certain boys can make a career of rugby or not. My criteria to discern a forward from a back (which is really generic for all coaches) is:

If he's chunky and temperamental, stick him in the forwards.
If he's small, well-groomed and can catch a ball, he is almost certainly a back.

Soon enough, these boys learn that there is a sharp division between a forward and a backline player. The forward thinks the backs look like fairies and act like parasites, enjoying the benefits of their good work. The backs think of their forwards as

7

---

[7] When the halfbacks split into differing functions, the one closest to the scrum became the scrum half but his colleague gathered several names – outside half, out half, stand-off half or just fly half. The name fly half came from Eton.

clumsy oafs with two left hands. For the sake of all team sports, they will play beside each other toward a common cause, but come the final whistle you could bet they were sworn enemies.

I've always wondered what people from non-rugby playing countries (most of the known world) must make of this game. Surely the lasting impression of a scrum is a couple of fatties having a big hug whilst the anonymous backline lurk somewhere behind having a chat. 'But these are all part of the fine subtleties and intricacies of rugby,' I would remind them.

Despite the simple folk that play the sport, rugby never has been a simple game: 'Seven varieties of football emerged from the common origin of pre-modern folk games. There is Association Football, two varieties of rugby and two North American mutations thereof, plus the creations born of Irish and Australian cultural resistance to British games.'[8] Today, about 120 countries play the sport. But don't be fooled: only about five of them stand a chance of ever winning the World Cup.

That's enough about rugby's genesis. More importantly; how did it emigrate to Africa's south?

EXODUS

Although the Rugby version eventually became the form of football adopted in South Africa, it was a modified Winchester

---

[8] Huw Richards, *A Game for Hooligans: the History of Rugby Union*, p. 16.

game that first gave birth to football on the southern tip of the continent. The first fields christened by the new game were those of the Diocesan College, the school more commonly known as Bishops, and the man responsible was Canon George Ogilvie, the school's headmaster from 1861-85.[9]

The first Anglican Bishop of Cape Town, Robert Gray, had founded two schools in his Bishopscourt home in 1849. One was for black pupils and the other for whites. But the home-schooling didn't last long and soon one moved onto the Zonnebloem Estate in the prosperous city, while the other became the Diocesan Collegiate School (Bishops) when it moved to the unprosperous farm of Woodlands – land once owned by Jan van Riebeeck. It was to Bishops that Grey sent George Ogilvie in 1861 to instil English public school discipline. And Ogilvie in turn introduced the belief – still prevalent in good education today – that sport was important to the development and discipline of boys. It wasn't all lip service either. The bearded headmaster participated with the boys, and only 'retired' from football at 54 years of age![10]

---

[9] Rugby football became more organised in 1871 when a football union was formed which adopted the laws as played at Rugby School – the Rugby Football Union, still the title of the body ruling the game in England. However, it was not until 1892 that the laws of the game became systemised. The claims, therefore, of any organisation to have been the first to play the Rugby game before 1892 are probably far-fetched. What they had was somebody's version of the game. At the Cape, people played Ogilvie's game till 1875 when Villagers played Hamiltons according to their version of the Rugby game. The Rugby game became more entrenched with the arrival of William Milton at the Cape and his involvement in Villagers. St Andrew's may have been playing their form of the game from 1876, certainly from 1878 when they played Graeme College. Hilton College would claim 1877, when Henry Vaughan Ellis became headmaster. The essential difference between the two games was that rugby allowed carrying the ball and tackling, but the lines between the codes were so blurred that when Paarl played Malmesbury in 1881, Malmesbury played by Rugby rules and Paarl by Association (soccer) rules. Malmesbury won. The various rugby unions were established primarily therefore to standardise the laws.

[10] It was then common for men and boys to participate together in sport, and age restrictions were virtually non-existent.

His rendition of the Winchester rules at Bishops was known as 'Gog's football' or 'Gogball' (Ogilvie's nickname was Gog), and that was the beginning of football's roots in South Africa.[11] However, by 1871 a football union had been founded, and it adopted the rules of Rugby School (soon to become the accepted norm). Ogilvie was not impressed by this, and when asked if Bishops would play by the Rugby rules, he grumbled, 'Well, if you boys want to kill yourselves, do so!'

Though Bishops may have unwillingly accepted the Rugby game, it is nevertheless credited as first bringing one of the forms of the game to South Africa. The game naturally spread thereafter, especially in places where there was a conglomeration of active young men, such as the mines in Johannesburg and Kimberley, but also at the growing number of schools at the time.

BISHOPS AND SOME RUGBY TRADITIONS

H H Castens, known as 'Fatty', was South Africa's first cricket captain to lead a team abroad, but he also played and captained

---

[11] Ogilvie's game was not referred to as the Winchester game because that would have implied rules specific to the Winchester school game (even varying field space dictated varying rules and versions). Being familiar with the Winchester game, Ogilvie adhered to many of its rules, but nevertheless introduced the game at Bishops as his version, thus making it Gog's football. SACS also played his game, as did South Africa's first football clubs – Hamiltons and Villagers.

the South African rugby team in its debut Test against the touring British in 1891, and he refereed the final Test of that same series! He was also the country's first great rugby coach, at a time when the coach's main job was to make sure everyone knew the rules. He coached Bishops and the Villagers club, who often practiced together on the Rondebosch Common, and set a precedent for 15-man rugby whereby all players should be capable of scoring tries.

Barry 'Ox' Heatlie, better known as 'Fairy' (rugby finds fantastic nicknames!) was perhaps the first rugby 'superstar' in South Africa. A massive, versatile and mobile rugby player, he was selected for the First XV upon arriving at Bishops, and captained South Africa in their first Test and series victory. Books could be written on his many achievements but certainly his most enduring legacy was the green Springbok jersey. The choice of green originated from the shirts of the Old Diocesan RFC, and was first proudly worn in the final Test against the touring British in 1896 (when they beat the tourists for the first time). South Africa wore the jersey again when they won a series for the first time in 1903. Heatlie was the captain. And the victory cemented the place of the green Springbok jersey.[12]

With many old boys representing South Africa and other nations (especially in the early years of the sport), Bishops has made an immense contribution to rugby. But it is the school's traditions that have I have always admired. From the game's fundamentals – that were taught with an aim to preparing boys

---

[12] The colours of jerseys were tractable till the introduction of gaudy, designer jerseys and the addition of numerous advertisements. Jerseys were initially dependent on the fabric and dyes available. White was the commonest colour, and then came one-colour jerseys. England's white jerseys came from Rugby School. South Africa chose green because Barry Heatlie, the captain, had a set of green jerseys, the colours of his club, the Old Diocesans RFC. Bishops played in dark blue because these tough jerseys were used by the labourers on ships and would last longer. SACS play in blue and white stripes because those were the only jerseys available in Cape Town at the time. They then became the Western Province colours. Natal took its black and white from Hilton College.

for life beyond school – to Webb Ellis's running tradition, Bishops has always maintained the essence of what rugby originally stood for. Those avoiding hibernation on wintry Saturday mornings in the Cape to see Bishops take to the field will testify to this.

But it was a midweek game at Bishops – and the first home game of the season (against the visiting St Andrew's College of Grahamstown) – which I was now on my way to watch. Arriving at the iron memorial gates of the Diocesan College – which today is in the heart of leafy Rondebosch – the sound of rasping mothers and the smell of boerewors rolls led me up the avenue, guarded either side with stone pines, to the derby unfolding on the Piley Rees field.[13] I was here to meet a legendary Bishops coach and one of its 60-odd Springboks.

Despite the chilly south-easterly, there's always a vocal crowd at the Piley Rees on derby day. At such occasions there is an unwritten law that all those in attendance – regardless of their knowledge of the game – are allowed to dispense lungfuls of advice from the safety of the touchline. The most common advice is 'tackle him!' and 'wake up!', and must be shouted in a way that assumes this was not on the players to-do list. The referee is also often the recipient of advice. It is always cynical and must show no regard for qualification or distinction. Only if your team wins has the ref offered even a vaguely satisfactory performance.

I join the swelling crowds on the sidelines nearest Table Mountain, well away from the boisterous old boy sections. On the opposite touchline sit the Bishops boys, clad in blue blazers, and behind them looms the medieval-looking White House, one of three boarding houses at the school. The traditional curtain-raiser, the second-team game, was in progress when Basil Bey joined me.

Bey, a well-known name in the Cape (particularly in schools

---

[13] These days Bishops is an affluent private school, and it is difficult to imagine that it began in a humble cottage with six pupils.

rugby), is a coach from a bygone era – an era before it all became too serious. Reared in Rhodesia, he settled in Cape Town during his time at UCT – where he was in no rush to qualify as a teacher (he was there from 1956-63) – and after successful coaching stints, most notably at False Bay RFC and Bishops, he still keeps his hands muddied among the grassroots at Bishops.

Now into his 70s Bey's sharp green eyes – today under an aged blue Bishops cap – still sparkle with humour as he tells me how he ended up being involved with Bishops. 'I could have ended up at Rondebosch Boys', but I signed my application "Yours sincerely" instead of "Yours faithfully", which was frowned upon then,' Basil said with a wry smile. 'So I ended up at Bishops, coaching the juniors at first, and then the First XV from 1972 until 1998.'

Only 400 metres separates the two schools, however they have very different rugby histories. In fact, Rondebosch nearly abandoned rugby in its early years. In 1908 Rondebosch played its first rugby match against Bishops and lost 112-0. Painton Cowen, who played for Transvaal at the tender age of 19, scored 86 points that day. Rondebosch gave up rugby for the rest of the season, but soon returned to the game with far more success. Today, the Bishops-'Bosch fixture is a flourishing derby – the largest in the Cape Town area – and draws vociferous old boy support.

Bey was never shy to try something unconventional. Like the three-man scrum that would wheel a powerful opposition pack around when the loose head gave way, and create a possible turnover so that he could use his 12-man backline! And Bishops were also one of the first to use the shortened line-out. But the tradition for which Bishops is most renowned is that of running rugby. They prefer to see the ball purposefully floating among their players rather than hibernating beneath burrowing bodies.

'Many of the big Afrikaans schools thought of us as soft little

English boys, and that our forwards were weak.' Bey smiled. 'But we aimed to match them there, and then outplay them with our skills. I always said that "all kicks are bad kicks", and obviously that should be taken with a pinch of salt, but it's a good general policy to hold.

'As far as I know Bishops have played this way since the days of coach Castens. They certainly did when I watched them for the first time in Rhodesia in 1949. They beat Prince Edward 55-5. The very essence of rugby is running with the ball. Anyone can kick it away. So we coached the Bishops boys, from the prep to the high school, with the necessary skills to play a running game. That doesn't mean we neglected the scrum and other set pieces, of course. If anything, we worked even harder on those, so that we'd be able to run the ball more often.'

As the Bishops First XV team went into a composed huddle just beyond the rugby poles, Bey confided that he had never seen much point in long-winded lectures on tactics minutes before a game: 'The work has already been done, and anything more than "go out there and get on with it" is more than the boys can handle on a Saturday morning.'

Nor did Bey spend time working the boys up into a frothing emotional frenzy before the game. Even hugs and high fives were out. Dignified passion and respect for the game and its opponents were the cherished traditions and practice.

As they broke from their huddle I noticed that the all-blue Bishops First XV jerseys carried no numbers on their backs – the pious educational reasoning being that as rugby is a team game no individual ought to draw attention to himself. Numbering players was once a hot issue. When England first wore numbers at Twickenham on 18 March 1922, King George V, a keen rugby supporter, turned to the secretary of the Scottish Rugby Union, the conservative J. Aikman Smith, and said, 'I see England have numbers. What a good idea. When are Scotland going to get numbers?'[14]

In indignation Aikman Smith replied, 'Sire, my players are men, not cattle.' And the story is that he refused to speak to His Majesty for the rest of the afternoon.

I probed Basil for other rugby traditions institutionalised at the 160-year-old school.

'The senior players in the old days also used to wear caps and only took them off before the start of the game,' he told me. 'Rugby School started all that.'

Caps have always been a part of the game, and today indicate Test match appearances, and who gets to sit at the back of the team bus.[15] It is difficult to imagine a Victor Matfield making his way down the Ellis Park tunnel with a little green cap placed on

[14] Numbers, it is believed, were first used in 1897 in Brisbane when the New Zealanders played Queensland. 'As an experiment to assist spectators, a number will be placed on each player's back.' When they were brought to Sydney in 1904 players objected because it was too convenient a way for referees to identify miscreants. On 21 January 1922 numbers were used in a Five Nations match for the first time – when England played Wales at Cardiff Arms Park. The Springboks wore numbers on the 1906-07 tour, though not against Scotland. Their opponents sometimes wore numbers, eg Yorkshire, Middlesex, Newport and East Midlands. The Springboks wore tour numbers. Howard Marshall, for years the rugby correspondent of the *Daily Telegraph,* wrote in 1936 in an article entitled 'What Rugger Means to Me': 'Here I must make what is probably my last protest against the numbering of players. I remember how I resented this cattle-branding when I was playing myself, and my unholy delight when the numbered jerseys did not correspond with the programmes. Rugby football is not a game for such fripperies as numbering and programmes; it is not a game to be watched by any but those who have played it and understand it.' In 1933 soccer players were numbered at the FA Cup Final for the first time. Everton, who won, played Manchester City (Everton were numbered 1-11, Manchester City 12-22). Celtic still refuse to wear numbers on their backs. Sometimes teams have worn letters as there was a belief that a single letter was less confusing than two numbers. The famous English clubs Bristol and Leicester used letters from A to O till the advent of professionalism and TV exposure. Bristol had A at fullback, Leicester O at fullback. When they played it looked as if a whole lot of scrabble tiles had been flung onto the field.

[15] The idea of awarding caps comes from Rugby School. School House was the sporting heart of Rugby School and in 1839 when Queen Adelaide came to the school to watch a game of football, the team wore red velvet caps in her honour. The School House players wore white shirts and white shorts – which became England's colours in 1871 (when Rugby ruled the game in England).

his considerable mop today, but then as a staunch traditionalist, I'm glad to see many observances have remained in one way or another.

Just then Dave von Hoesslin arrived. I had asked the former Springbok scrum half to join us for some banter and offered to buy him a beer for every good story. He was notably early.

Dave played two seasons of First XV rugby, but it was the '92 side, arguably one of the best in the history of rugby at Bishops, that grew the crowds and interest. No wonder when you consider that the front row weighed more than the Western Province front row at the time, and that Selborne Boome, Von Hoesslin, Herschelle Gibbs (fly half) and Robbie Fleck (inside centre) all featured in the line-up.[16] The only game Bishops lost in that season was when Gibbs was playing for South African Schools at Newlands. Von Hoesslin, Boome and Fleck would later play for Western Province and make their national debut together against Italy in 1999.

Though Gibbs will be remembered for his cricketing exploits, he was also an incredibly talented rugby player. 'Gibbs was uncoachable,' Basil told me. 'You didn't need to coach him. Sometimes when you teach a certain child in the classroom, you realise that you're teaching someone who is much brighter than you. Herschelle was like that on the sports field, and certainly one of the most gifted rugby players I ever coached.'

'Could he have been a Bok instead of a Protea?' I asked.

---

[16] A steady flow of South Africa's finest stars passed under Bey's tutelage during his time at Bishops: Selborne Boome; Robbie Fleck; David von Hoesslin; Guy Kebble; Haldane Luscombe (of Wales), Stuart Abbott (of England); Daniel Vickerman (of Australia); Mark Burton-Moore; Bob Bolus; Dirk Hoffman; Herschelle Gibbs; Adrian Kuiper; Andrew Campbell and many more, including Michael Ehrentraut. He came to Bishops having never played rugby. He began in the u14E team and worked his way up to the Bishops First XV, and became the Western Province and South African Schools captain in 1989. He was a fullback who scored 48 tries and 424 points in 62 matches for Bishops. He had become a goal-kicker halfway through 1988 when he scored 245 points, only 27 of them from penalties. He now resides in Australia.

'Absolutely. There were things he could do that I have never seen other players do. I remember a game where he was taking a 22 dropout. He restarted with a drop to the opposition 22, but it was such a high kick that by the time one of the opposition had gathered the ball the Bishops chasers were already tackling him. I can also remember that on a trip to Grahamstown we stopped in Sedgefield for the night. A game of darts had begun, and Herschelle, having never played the game before, promptly began throwing bullseyes with each throw. But I think it was other things that made him an unbelievable player. Like that match in Grahamstown against St Andrew's. They were our traditional rivals, and it had been a tense, hard game but we had come out on top. Of course, Herschelle had had a great game, but after the match I found him standing in a corner alone with his head against his arms that were pressed on the wall. I thought he was injured and went to find out what the matter was. But he was crying; just so overjoyed with the win and the occasion. That really warmed my heart. He always had the right attitude, despite all the things that are written about him today. He's a great team man and has a fantastic sense of humour. But when anyone told him how good he was, he'd start a different conversation. He was humble, and an example of how rugby players should conduct themselves.'

Gibbs' teammate Dave von Hoesslin had followed in his father's footsteps and completed his five-year boarding sentence at School House. Making beds with hospital corners and doing the mandatory fagging duties was par for the course, but Dave had a few stories on Bishops traditions to share that were not the mandatory boarding school mischief.

Each year the matrics from the three boarding houses take part in something called 'fighting for the lion' – a tradition that has been around for almost as long as the school has. Fighting for the lion entails one boarding house (the one which is in possession of the lion – a glorified teddy bear, I presumed) 'parading' it to

17

the other two boarding houses at a set time and place – normally the top rugby fields at midnight. There, the matrics will meet and use any means necessary to retrieve and return the lion to their own boarding house. This happens probably once a term. When the 'meeting' takes place, the lion will be brought out and a wrestling match will ensue among the bigger guys, while all the faster (or fairer) guys wait near the action in the hope that one of his housemates will manage to wrestle the lion free and throw it to him (a bit like the original version of rugger, really). Thereafter it becomes a race to see whether some desperate soul has the legs to make it to the safety of his house. If he is hauled in and 'tackled' the ruck will resume until the lion is wrestled free once more. When someone finally manages to escape, with lion intact, to his house, this is considered the end of the fight. Until the next one. Possession of the lion brings bragging rights, but it is the house photographed with it at the end of the year – with the lion enjoying pride of place in front of the boys – which finally settles the matter (and some even swear the lion breaks out into a wry smile moments before the flash).

Dave was once sitting down to enjoy his breakfast in the house when in rushed the boarders from Founders House hell-bent on a lion raid – there had been a lion fight the evening before and the lion was being proudly displayed on the trophy shelf in the breakfast room. The boys, probably in youthful glee, were running along the tables with food and cutlery going everywhere. All this time, the unperturbed housemaster at the head table gave attention only to his Kellogg's. Although fighting for the lion is not 'legal' it has been so traditionalised that for the most part the teachers at Bishops just turn a blind eye.

But Dave was once deprefected over the tradition. A new headmaster arrived in his final year at Bishops, and as Dave and a few others made haste from the scene of a lion fight (via the headmaster's garden) the man himself strode out and cornered Dave and his luckless crew, all kitted out in their rugby gear.

Deprefecting the lot of them on the spot, he then demanded that the boys hand in the lion the following morning. It amounted to a deliberate attempt to end the tradition. Instead, a lion made of papier mâché was created and the lion survived to be torn and mangled another day.

Basil once tried to find the origin of fighting for the lion – in yearbooks and so forth – but he told me that he could find no recorded history anywhere, probably because it's never been official. Perhaps it's the root of Bishops' rugby success? If boys can risk life and limb for a maned teddy bear, imagine what happens when you toss a rugby ball to one of them.

A shrill whistle blast announced the end of the second-team game. Dave glanced toward the Bishops First XV, now standing in a single line, ready for battle. Beyond them was the school's impressive whitewashed chapel that rose above the surrounding classrooms. There is another hushed Bishops tradition known as 'breaking into the chapel'. Once a year the boys would break into the vestry of the chapel and then climb into the roof. Each would hang a school tie from the rafters and write their names on the ceiling as well as in a book that is up there. It's a dangerous exercise and one which many a teacher has tried to put an end to, but each year the boys determinedly manage to find a way in there. When it was Dave's turn to break in he discovered the ties and names of both his father and uncle.

St Andrew's, a fine rugby school which has always been the traditional rival of Bishops, made their way onto the pitch.[17] Then the Bishops side jogged on, though between the poles nearest to the school. A partisan roar welcomed them. Basil discerned my confused frown at the unusual entrée. 'That began at the St Stithian's Festival, the first Easter festival that began in the early 80s. We were playing the hosts, who had Lance Sherrell

---

[17] The Anglican school rivals first began playing each other in 1896. Many at Bishops believe this game, more so than the Rondebosch fixture, to be the traditional rivalry.

in their line-up. But just before the game had begun, a long, antagonistic line of home support had gathered on the halfway line for the teams to run between. I didn't see why there had to be such emotion and hype before the game had even begun, and thought the boys would just lose their focus. I told them to run onto the field from the poles, and that tradition has just remained.'

'No school song, haka, or team huddle on the pitch before kick-off, either,' I observed as the St Andrew's fly half readied himself.

'No. Which I like. I never wanted my teams to make the opposition wait while they did those things. A touring New Zealand team, I think in '95, were furious when we began playing some touch rugby while they did their haka! Some Bishops parents weren't too happy with me either after that, and maybe it was a bit too much, but the fact is, teams should have done all their prep, team talks and all the rest of it before they get onto the field. The field is there for the match. That's what the spectators have come to watch. I don't think there should be wild celebrations after a try has been scored either. That's disrespectful to your opposition.'

Basically, Basil prefers everything to be as unsoccerish as possible.

'Piley Rees,' he said as the fly half moved to make his kick, 'would always say just before the start, and with pipe in mouth: "Play rugby, Bishops." He expected to see ball-in-hand rugby.'

Bishops, as is their custom, did just that. The boys in blue found their running rhythm easily, and with a noticeable lack of 'schoolboy errors' both forwards and backs combined to score some fine tries, so that by the half-time whistle Bishops had built a fair lead over their opponents.

The days of sucking on oranges at half-time are long over. Now an army of first years attack their First XV with bottles containing energade and kryptonite.

Whistle. Soaring restart. Gather. And the ball was shifted wide once more.

Passionate defence and some great handling and attacking play were the features of the second half. It was impressive considering how early in the season it was. Or was it? Seasons are starting earlier with each new year. Many First XV's now begin conditioning and training in November in preparation for preseason tours and Easter festivals. Many choose summer sports such as rowing that will complement the long winter season.

A long whistle blast ended the game. A few heads dropped in disappointment and exhaustion, but all around the ground those who had come to watch offered hearty and appreciative applause for their efforts.

Bishop had won an exciting rugby match between two fine rugby sides from two fine schools. Both teams had come to play rugby as it should be played. The crowd appreciated it, and the Bishops boys encircled their First XV to congratulate them on their heroics. It is on this stage – on the Piley Rees – that most of these players are likely to play their greatest and most memorable rugby.

Leaving Basil and Dave to catch up with old friends, I joined those making their way hastily up the avenue to beat the traffic. There were still some boys on the reserve fields beside the avenue, blissfully oblivious of the titanic derby that had been played only yards away. One undersized kaalvoet youngster, with a jersey down to his ankles and headgear drooping over his eyes, broke away from the rest of his peers and tore down the field clutching a melon-sized rugger ball. He threw his tiny frame over some imaginary try line, sliding over a muddied, trodden corner. It dawned on his two team mates that a try has been scored and wild celebrates commenced, while their opponents argued that it was the wrong imaginary try line. The game holds a purity at this level that can offer an altogether different entertainment to that saturated upon our screens. Like those u10 games where the young oaf with pubescent stubble, who his teammates refer to as 'Slobberchops' or 'Hercules', swats away the slothful efforts of his opponents as he strides towards the try line yet again. It's in these years that rugby's spirit is instilled and nurtured at the old traditional school that is Bishops. It's in these years that the boys are taught to play the game as it should be played, and that even a rare breed of forward is developed: one who can run and think at the same time.

In the very first school magazine, published in 1886, an anonymous letter writer complains that the rugby games he had seen were 'simply displays of brute strength, lacking altogether in skill and strategy'. How often is this, over 120 years on, still a familiar criticism within South African rugby? Though South Africa may possess a surplus of brute strength that has naturally inclined it to 'the hooligan's game', it is the brain, heart and imagination that ultimately make the game distinct. It is the thinking man's game, after all, and has to remain so.

Bishops – South African rugby's Garden of Eden – had remained obedient to the game's very essence. The rugby genesis began in a school, and so I thought it appropriate that I had begun there as well. Now – after a brief sojourn in the Winelands – I would be making my way east along the Garden Route to the Eastern Cape. From there it would be the trek north – Bloemfontein, KwaZulu-Natal, Pretoria and Joburg – with a UK stint for good measure and good rugby. On my travels I was hoping to meet proud rugby people as diverse as the many cultures of this country and to uncover the spirit of the game that unites them.

BRING BACK THE TOUR

Meanwhile ... [*ominous growing drum beat begins*] ... some distance north, among the dark Mountains of Mordor, Orcs and Englishmen and other foul creatures have been gathering to plot the downfall of the Land of the Bok (with its overgrown Hobbits and muscular Elves, and so forth).

The invasion is imminent.

Legions of foreign foes have been plotting and planning, and stirring up fear. [*Stage grows steadily darker and the drum is beating at a mad and frenetic pace now.*]

There is even nonsense speak of defeating the bearers of ... the Webb Ellis Ring! [*Thunderclap climax!*]

The British and Irish Lions tour is perhaps the game's biggest tradition. It is a tour that evokes true rugby spirit, and though it harks back to the old days it continues to thrive in the professional era. The Lions tour is refreshing. It breaks from the monotony of the tours that the Springboks endure at the end of each year in order to suit broadcaster requirements. Now the Lions will visit nearly every major rugby center in South Africa. From Rustenburg to Cape Town, and Bloemfontein to Port Elizabeth, the Lions will engage with the country's rugby communities and promote the development of the game.

In these professional days, traditional tours are often lifeless, but the Lions tour is different. Bitter English and Celtic rivalries are put aside for two months every four years, as a common southern hemisphere enemy unites a crusading team. A Lions series is like being awakened from a deep slumber and brought back to reality – to the reality of the amateur tradition. My quest (honestly, an excuse to do a road trip with a few rugby games thrown in) would culminate with the third Lions Test in July 2009.

Clutching an old Dictaphone, a dog-eared copy of *Tom Brown's Schooldays* and a bag stuffed with as many clean clothes as I could muster, I began my trek, aiming my rusty green Golf for Paarl.

II

LOOKING EAST

Grey High School

May – June 2008

THE WINELANDS

The quintessential Cape experience takes place in the surrounds of a vineyard. This is where the wine hacks gather to dop matured vintages and discuss the *oakiness* and *texture* of their chosen glass tipple. For the connoisseur of fine rugby, however, there is also plenty to be savoured in the local clubs and schools of the small towns scattered across the Boland.

It is remarkable that the South African papers barely give schools' rugby enough column inches for a smudgy reference (somewhere between softball and netball) when you consider that the annual Paarl Interskole – between Paarl Boys' High and Paarl Gimnasium – attracts 25,000 people each year. That's more than most provincial games and often more than the Western Province game taking place on the same day just down the road (and it's no surprise then that the local union have on occasion asked the Paarl schools to shift their kick-off a little earlier in the day). Derbies between two local schools are always the most intense of rugby battles, with the victor receiving the bragging rights until next they meet. Close proximity will always add healthy needle to a competition. Pretoria Boys and Affies lads could happily throw stones at each other for break-time amusement. So too could DHS and Glenwood, the three old Grahamstown schools and their two Kroonstad neighbours,

Rooiskool and Blouskool.

But the Paarl derby is especially significant. Unless you have sampled it, it is hard to imagine how the sleepy valley, spread with tranquil vineyards, is transformed by a bustling, excited town anticipating its grandest calendar date: Interskole. This is a day that begins long before the First XV kick off. In fact, the First XV game is the culmination of a week of festivities as raucous old boys are reunited from every nook and cranny and the local shops on the long, straight Main Road are draped in the lively colours of the schools (most shops display *both* schools' colours to maintain their full quota of customers). Finally, when the old boy games are finished, all other teams and sports have played their part and the ceremony in which the fathers hand over the First XV caps to each of their sons is also over, the crowds descend.

The swollen numbers dictate that the schools themselves cannot host this fixture. Instead, the gates of the neutral Paarl Rugby Grounds in Faure Street are opened to the multitude, and with it an army of paparazzi-like photographers and a bevy of television cameras. The programmes are either blue or green, and you need to choose wisely. You are either a Gimmie or a Boishaaier, or in more unflattering terms, a 'Bloedwors' or a 'Galpil'.[18] Lord help the Gimmie who wears blue underpants during Interskole week or the Boishaaier with green bootlaces. Prior to the game cheerleaders prance about, parading bloated mugshots of each player, parachutists descend upon the pitch clad in the colours of their allegiances and the school bands blare away on electric keyboards and guitars, belting out their favourite school songs. It may irk some of the traditionalists, but there's no doubting the crowd it draws.

The First XV game is the fitting finale to what has gone before and when it eventually gets underway it is rarely disappointing. And *very* rarely has one side run away with victory since they

---

[18] 'Bloedwors' is blood sausage. 'Galpil' is a bitter pill.

first began battering each other in 1915.[19] A victor is never guaranteed before kick-off and many a dream team has been dealt a nightmarish return. Extra skill and breath is somehow conjured up till the final seconds of what will be the biggest rugby occasion in most of these boys' lives – lose every match but win the First XV game and you have won Interskole! It's like watching two siblings who have grown up competing with one another, but though the siblings are close enough – Boishaai in the south of the town and Gimmies just a little further north – they have vastly different stories to tell.

It was in Paarl that the impetus to have Afrikaans recognised as an official language first began, and Paarl Gim was instrumental in this. In 1866 a Dutchman by the name of Arnoldus Pannevis arrived at Gim to teach Latin and Greek. One of the pupils he influenced was S. J. du Toit. Dominee Du Toit founded the Genootskap van Regte Afrikaners with its Afrikaans mouthpiece *Die Afrikaanse Patriot*.[20] Paarl Gim was central to this movement – necessitated because the Cape then belonged to England and moves were being made to anglicise the Afrikaners – and played a pivotal role in laying the foundations of modern Afrikaans (it is also the reason the Taal Monument is at Paarl).[21]

On 12 January 1858 Paarl Gim opened with five pupils, supported by the public and the Dutch Reformed Church. However, it wasn't until 40 years later – in the mid-1890s – that the pupils asked the principal for permission to found a rugby club at the school. His response was to tell them to work in the garden if they wanted exercise. The boys were obviously

[19]   Fixtures between the two were played earlier than 1915, though the results recorded remain disputed to say the least. The largest margin of victory between the two is only 20 points, perhaps the smallest margin of any long-standing rivalry in South African schools rugby. It was a 20-0 victory to Paarl Gimnasium in 1920.

[20]   Incidently, Dominee Du Toit's son was apparently born in the old biology classroom. He would be the famous poet *Totius* (Jacob Daniel du Toit).

[21]   In 1925, Afrikaans became an official language of South Africa in the place of Dutch.

undeterred though, because a decade later there were four Paarl Gim old boys in Paul Roos' Springbok team of 1906-07 (the first to be coined 'Springbokken'). Those were the days when the school played rugby upon a vlei and when the principal, F. C. Wal, captained the First XV! Since then, Paarl Gimnasium has produced a steady flow of mature Boks, and in 1983 two World Cup-winning Boks, Balie Swart and Kobus Wiese, were part of a hefty Gim pack. Ever the philosophers, they began to work out how they could take advantage of playing rugby in the pouring rain should such weather conditions prevail at Interskole. Their 'research' was concluded with the discovery that they were able to handle the ball far better when wearing the 'inners' of cricket gloves. Interskole was indeed wet that year and coach Pine Pienaar allowed them to don their 'Jackson' gloves.

In that '83 Gim side was also a future WP fly half by the name of Riaan Gous. He religiously practiced his goal-kicking but each painstaking place, pause, gaze and kick required a fresh sandcastle to be laboriously moulded. Taking the lead from his pack, he decided that he would invent a latex kicking tee at a time when the known rugby world knew only of sand buckets. Staunch right-wing opposition and a few Neanderthal referees would have none of this cocky, sandless misinvention though, and rubbished the idea with the same scorn as they reserved for the 'five-point try'.[22]

Another ingenious way of enhancing your performance on the pitch is called the cane. Or the rod. Or the plank. Or the lash. And many other such welcoming names. Of course, this

[22] The use of the kicking tee in rugby was the brainchild of Don Burgess. While attending Western Washington University, in the early 1950s, he was the kicker for the football team and attempted to introduce its use into his rugby games in British Columbia during that time, but without success. Years later, in 1987, he realised that kickers at the first World Cup would only be using sand, and he sought to develop the first model of the kicking tee in 1988. He asked the International Rugby Board for permission to trial it in Canada, to which they responded: 'Go ahead.' Of course, it was successful and today Don's company have patented numerous designs to avoid competitors and maintain official IRB approval.

fine 'instrument of education' has long been banned – much to the frustration of housemasters and rugby coaches across the country.[23] However, if you happened to be a member of the Paarl Gim u15A side in 1996, as Bok centre Jean de Villiers was, then you are decidedly old school, for it was that team that insisted upon the reinstatement of the cane to enhance their performances. They even gave it a name: Daisy. For the next two years Daisy would see to it that concentration levels were at an all-time peak, and that no rugby ball was ever dropped. Unsurprisingly, the team went unbeaten for two years, and I am still holding thumbs that Jean de Villiers may have a quiet word with his Bok coach regarding the merits of introducing the cane into the practices of our national team.

Gim did not have the monopoly on sneaky coaching tactics, however. Boishaai has had many fine coaches, and one in particular, Tom Engela, certainly had some unique ideas. Once, his u16A pre-season training was devoid of rugby balls, the coach preferring to use bricks instead. The reasoning being that with bricks flying about a boy will *always* be prepared, with his hands up and ready to receive a pass at all times. The boys may have felt rather red-faced when their peers christened them the Baksteen Brigade (Brick Brigade), but when they began producing scintillating running rugby, culminating in a 16-3 victory at Interskole, there may well have been more than one coach who considered a wheelbarrow full of bricks more useful than a bag of rugby balls.

Another Engela tactic was to take a coin out of his pocket during his pre-match team talk and inform his young side that this would be his 'connection to the team on the field'. After asking each member of the team to handle the coin, he would then place it back in his pocket. There it would remain for the entire match; his hand clutching it tightly. He had warned the eager-to-please laaitjies that each time they made a wrong decision or

31

---

[23] The cane was banned in South Africa in 1994.

an error, the coin would burn his hand. During the match many an anxious boy would glance at their coach on the sidelines to see if his hand would leave his pocket, but it never did. How many times his palm and fingers were burnt, the boys never knew, but their performances were almost always inspirational.

In its earlier days, Boishaai's only field was also its playground. With 18 teams trying to make use of this space during afternoon rugby practices, the unwary were warned in 1933 that the field was 'a *danger* to both young and old'. The school arrived a decade after the private, church-owned Paarl Gimnasium was founded. Boishaai, however, was established by the government and lessons were in English. As with all schools back then, the early days were hard work, and teachers and headmasters were few and far between. And when they did finally arrive by ox cart, they did not stay long. Still, famous coaches and old boys crossed paths. One Irishman who was instrumental in developing organised sport at Boys' High was Billy Middleton.[24] He taught maths at the school from 1901 to 1933 and was an enthusiastic member of Paarl Rugby Club – so enthusiastic in fact that he was known to miss a bit of school in the week following a home victory, such was his penchant for celebration.

On one occasion Boys' High beat SACS to win the u17 shield at Newlands. They came back to Paarl in a happy frame of mind and were marching down the main street singing when Middleton came charging out of a bar. He grabbed one of the boys, Jim Fouché – the future state president – by the arm and dragged him into the bar. Before the assembled drinkers he said: 'My boy, please, let us into your happy secret. Just tell us the good news – that you beat SACS today.'

But Fouché remained silent.

Middleton said: 'Then just you and I shall sing "God Save the King".'

---

[24] In 1939 Middleton was made a life member of the Western Province RFU, a rare honour.

Again Fouché was silent.

Then Middleton said: 'Or rather let us sing the school song. Just you and I.'

There, on a Saturday evening in a bar in Paarl, the teacher and the pupil stood to attention and sang the school song.

THE BURGERS

To get a word in with a Springbok can often entail navigating your way through a minefield of journalists or admirers, often only to receive some well-worn cliché for your efforts. But I had been invited to Burger HQ – Welbedacht wine farm near Wellington – to spend some time with the family in a more relaxed and informal setting.

As I left Paarl, on the Wellington road, the sun was beginning to set and by the time I began to ascend the farm road – the old Cape Dutch house in the distance – it was busy conjuring autumnal reds and oranges from the rolling vineyards. Parking in front of the lush lawn, onto which two thatched, whitewashed houses opened their doors, I marvelled at the magnificent setting – the tranquil dam, the manicured cricket oval behind the main house and the sprawling vineyards beyond.

A short while later the Land Rover of Schalk Senior rolled in and the large man climbed out to welcome me with a steady handshake. His mitts were huge and I immediately pitied his offspring – whose backsides must have felt the wrath of those paddles at some point.

Senior took me to into the house that stood beside their main residence – the Burgers were busy renovating and he wanted to check up on the enormous brick fireplace set in the far corner of the empty building, which he had designed.[25]

'Fireplaces are complex things, you know,' he muttered, his hands clutching upon brick and mortar as his head disappeared within.

I nodded agreeably, though I didn't know.

With Senior satisfied with the fireplace's progress we moved into the expansive lounge in the main house. Schalk Junior was on a neighbour's farm, hitting golf balls and perhaps tackling oak trees. 'He's on his way, though,' Senior reassured me.

Whilst the dogs vigorously licked themselves and each other at my feet, I pushed Senior for some thoughts on his son and the reputation he inherited from his father.

'I never pushed Schalkie into rugby,' Senior corrected me. 'We never even had rugby photos up in the house; I never wanted the old man to be looking down upon him. The only sport I ever insisted upon was golf. I've always thought golf is the sport closest to life, because you first have to play against yourself.'

Senior may be an imposing presence but he holds a rural sincerity about him, and as with any proud father he glows when speaking of his son's achievements. 'He was the first Matie to play First XV rugby and First XI cricket in his first year,' Senior said. 'And he was the first to play in two rugby World Cups in the same year, both in 2003, captaining the u21s and later joining Straeuli's ill-fated Boks in Australia. The next year he was voted the IRB Player of the Year.'

The accolades seemed to summon Junior because moments later the blond-mopped Schalk strode into the living room. In baggies and slops, he looked happy and relaxed as he shook my hand and flopped back onto one of the couches.

---

[25] The house was built in 1780.

From the moment Schalk Burger debuted for the Boks, he captured every rugby lover's heart – his ferocious tackling and enthusiasm for the game brought respect from supporter and opponent alike. With flashing blond hair and a cheeky smile, he is some rogue firework born for the dark arts of the flanker; a broad-shouldered breath of fresh air in this sport of gladiatorial professionalism. There are surely few that have consistently given as much in a game of rugby.

'His work rate and tackling were always the hallmark of his game,' Senior continued. 'Even at school, he would often do the work of many of his teammates. He was fiercely competitive. The Paarl Interskole played a big role there as well. It is an enormous stage for a schoolboy. I can even remember joining the old boys after one game and singing the school song together as a 10-year-old Schalkie pulled on my trousers and said, "I want to go to this school one day."'

I quiz the Burgers on what they think about the changes in the game; how its values and ethos may have changed from when Senior played in the amateur days.

'I just love the game,' Senior began. 'But every bloke that takes charge wants to change it, and that disrespects the past Anton Rupert said, "He who doesn't value and respect his past will have no future." What makes certain rugby countries great is their tradition, and many countries would love to have South Africa's rugby tradition. Under Craven, we were world leaders. There was ongoing improvement under his leadership. We tend to want to play like France or New Zealand, but we just need to play like ourselves, to our strengths. That is when we are at our best. But then, being a farmer, I've got a lot of time to think about these things!'

Though Junior may be among the highest earners in the Springbok team – with Bok and provincial contracts, as well as some major sponsors' deals – he is insistent that he still only plays the game because he enjoys it. And the coming Lions series really gets his juices flowing. 'I loved watching all the Lions games in '97, and attended the first Test at Newlands,' he said. 'You only get one opportunity, if you're lucky, to play the Lions. It's the greatest tour, with so much history and so much interest. Hopefully we're still going strong by the time the series arrives.'

So what will he do when his body no longer wishes to hunt down gangly fly halfs and oval balls? I asked.

'I'm really not sure yet,' he replied with a grin. 'But what I do know is that there'll be no more competitive sport after rugby.'

Fair enough. His is a body that's been battered more than most in this hooligan's game.[26]

THE HOOLIGAN'S GAME

Elizabeth Taylor once spoke for many when she said: 'I prefer rugby to soccer. I enjoy the violence in rugby, except when they start biting each other's ears off.'

If the Hooligan Rugby Rankings are ever compiled, a few notorious names would certainly arise. Colin Meads, the towering All Black lock, was once described as 'the kind of player you expect to see emerging from a ruck with the remains of a jockstrap between his teeth.'[27]

---

[26] The Schalk Junior experience includes two knee operations, two broken ribs, two neck operations, torn ligaments, a broken nose on numerous occasions and facial lacerations. And still counting.

[27] Quote by Sir Anthony O'Reilly.

Known as 'Pinetree', Meads would surely be near the top of the list. The farmer's training was (mythically) said to include ascending hills with a sheep tucked beneath each arm. What was undeniable was the trail of broken limbs and battered bodies he left in his wake, be they those of the opposition or those of his own countrymen. But his notoriety as one of the most violent men to ever play the hooligan's game was cemented by his treatment of the hapless Australian scrum half Ken Catchpole. With the Aussie pinned at the bottom of a ruck, Meads took hold of a protruding limb and proceeded to wrench him off the ball. The result was horrific. Catchpole's hamstring muscle stretched like a rubber band before snapping clean off the bone. And that was the end of Catchpole's rugby career, arguably the Aussies' finest ever scrum half.

Beyond a sending off against Scotland, no real punishment ever did seem to result from Meads' dark deeds, and, like Schalk Junior, he remained immensely popular among his peers and opponents (though perhaps to a lesser extent in Australia). He was a folk hero who personified the rugged New Zealand rugby of the day. He never warmed up before a game, stating that the haka was all he needed, and he never could comprehend how someone could want to be paid to wear the silver fern. Like Schalk Senior, Meads was from another era in every way.[28]

Two others from Middle Earth are also worth their place on the list.

All Black 'Red' Conway broke a finger whilst touring South Africa in 1960. The bone wouldn't knit and the injury was jeopardizing his tour. No matter, he just had it amputated.

Then there was Wayne 'Buck' Shelford – of a more recent All Black vintage but of an even meaner disposition. In 1986, in a brutal game against the French that would later be christened

[28] On the All Blacks 1970 tour to South Africa Meads' arm was brutally broken in a ruck when the tour was still young. He did, however, manage to return for the final two Tests, but retired a year later after 15 seasons of All Black rugby.

the 'Battle of Nantes', Shelford found himself at the bottom of a ruck, where rugby's darkest sins are committed. A Les Bleus stud somehow found its way to his groin where it tore his scrotum, leaving a testicle dangling out. As the physio stitched it up, the full extent of the churling injury was caught by an eager cameraman. Perhaps more shocking was that Buck had the balls to return to the pitch. He later said, 'I was knocked out cold, lost a few teeth and had a few stitches down below. It's a game I still can't remember . . . I don't really want to, either.' New Zealand lost 16-3.

Hulking Blair Mayne was a fierce Viking of a rugby player, a temperamental man capable of incredibly violent outbursts. The Irishman was prone to throwing teammates through hotel windows and daring anyone (or any group) to a bar fight. In 1938, while staying in Cape Town (the first two Tests of the Lions tour were played in the Mother City), he would dress in a seaman's jersey and make his way down to the Cape Town docks. With Welsh hooker Bill Travers by his side, they would wait for a foolish soul to mutter a derogatory comment in their direction. Then all hell broke loose as their *party* got underway.

The outbreak of World War II may have interrupted Mayne's rugby career, but it only enhanced his fierce reputation. Labelled 'a fighter of satanic ferocity', he often engaged Nazi troops in hand-to-hand combat to ensure his unit's safety.[29] He was once ordered to infiltrate a German airbase and blow up the aircraft there. Mayne slipped in stealthily and with a single blade killed 17 Nazis, each of whom was guarding a separate plane. He personally destroyed 130 German and Italian aircraft in raids into enemy territory in North Africa and at one stage had Rommel infuriated enough to send 10,000 troops to comb the desert in search of him and his troops. Blair Mayne became Britain's most decorated soldier of the war. If there was ever a man created for combat, it was probably him. Indeed, if there was ever a man made for the hooligan's game, it was certainly him.

38

---

[29] As aptly described by David Stirling, who founded the SAS.

While most rugby players don't have the combat experience of Blair Mayne, we have all watched more than our fair share of on-pitch thuggery.[30] However, perhaps the most famous such instance of thuggery was the '74 Lions tour. Before a ball had even been kicked, the touring Lions accused us of our own brand of thuggery. Impossible! We were the *hosts*! They thus declared thuggery *first*, and if one of their number had so much as his pants pulled down or his hair tugged they responded by shouting '99!'[31] The handbags came out in unison and, without fear of retribution from the ref, the Lions klapped the nearest unsuspecting Bok. This was completely unsportsmanlike as the Boks were not only losing the actual rugby games, but also getting bullied for their sins as well.

Many remember 'the call to arms' in the third Test which had fullback J P R Williams galloping 50 yards to take a swing at Bok bully Moaner van Heerden.

A few steps had to be taken to keep the Lions' testosterone in check off the pitch as well. After flooding the lobby, trashing the furniture and setting off the fire extinguishers of one particular Port Elizabeth hotel, the irate manager sought out captain Willie John McBride. On his fifth Lions tour and holding 19 Lions caps, the Ulster farmer was perhaps the finest Lion of them all. And certainly one of the toughest.

'Mr McBride, your players are wrecking my hotel,' the manager blurted out, bursting into the captain's room to find him in his underwear.

'Are there many dead?' asked McBride, taking a puff on his pipe.

---

[30] The word 'thug' is deriving from the Hindi word 'thag', meaning a swindler or a thief. However, it was more commonly used to refer to a sect of organised criminals in India who first befriended their victims before leading them into a slaughter. The sect was eventually eradicated by the British in the 1830s.

[31] 99 is a shortening of 999, which in Britain and Ireland is the phone number for the emergency services such as the police, ambulance or fire brigade.

'I want every one of you locked up; the police are on their way,' screamed the manager.

Weighing up the proposition, Willie John responded with a wry smile. 'Tell me,' he said. 'These police of yours – will there be many of them?'

Some have said that rugby is gladiatorial ballet: majestically sublime yet so brutal at the same time. Yet the brutality, and certainly the thuggery, is becoming increasingly rare. Not too long ago you could get away with thumping your opponent in the line-out when the ref wasn't looking. It was seen as a healthy and accepted part of this physical game. But with the advent of professionalism, such 'untoward and irresponsible behaviour' could now spell disaster for the assets of wealthy unions, and is subject to the harshest of punishments. Just recall the result of one of the worst misdemeanours in the modern era: Johan le Roux truly mistakes Sean Fitzpatrick's ear for cauliflower, and in the sanctity of the scrum he has more than a nibble of it. Fitzy was not impressed, and neither was Le Roux after being handed an 18-month suspension: 'For that suspension, I should have torn it off,' Le Roux said afterwards. 'Then at least I could say, "Look, I've returned to South Africa with the guy's ear."'

The stringent laws still catch out one or two of the ancient front-row buggers who learnt their game in traditional amateur clubs, but many would declare that the hooligan's game is becoming far more of a gentleman's game these days. And yet, when Schalk Burger and his ilk are roaming the veld you are reminded that perhaps the game still does enjoy some of its original thuggery – even though these days most of the handbagging is done out of sight of the ref (now that's professionalism!).

After not refusing the Burgers' offer to leave with a few bottles of Welbedacht's finest, I exited the farm gates. Across the rolling vineyards an old university town awaited, and no rugby quest would be complete without some time spent on the open fields of Stellenbosch.

THREE WISE MEN

Stellenbosch, the country's second-oldest town, was founded in 1679 by the governor Simon van der Stel and named after him. It is a beautiful town, graced with shady oaks and gazed upon by high mountains. It is also has a distinct cultural heritage with its Cape Dutch architecture and its pride in the Afrikaans language – the centrepiece of which is Stellenbosch University.

Although Stellenbosch University may owe its genesis to the very English Victoria College (later to become Paul Roos Gimnasium), as the nineteenth century passed so its will became increasingly bent on establishing an Afrikaner identity and culture. Rugby soon became an integral part of that and the town's first rugby club had already been established by 1880.[32]

Stellenbosch University and Paul Roos share the same colour rugby jersey – the maroon jersey with the gold collar and cuffs. It is the students, however, that 'borrowed' from the school. I was to meet with a man who had coached upon both the fields of the university and school, and who knew the great Danie Craven better than most. This is, after all, the town where Paul Roos, Oubaas Markötter and Doc Craven left indelible marks upon so many, including Springbok Dawie Snyman.

Born to a Dutch Reformed minister and baptised at that famous nursery of talent, Grey College in Bloemfontein, Snyman went on to earn caps for Western Province and the Springboks.

---

[32] Although Stellenbosch take the date from their oldest club photo (1880), they were certainly playing in 1878 and while labelling the club as an Afrikaans club is perhaps not entirely fair (Afrikaans was not yet recognised as a language), the club did have numerous Dutch members. Incidentally, a few years later (in 1882) the Roslyns Rugby Club of District Six had become South Africa's first non-white rugby club.

But his greatest influence has been at his beloved Stellebosch University, where his involvement has spanned four decades, beginning in 1974.

I had arranged to meet Dawie at his Pam Golding offices in the heart of the student town. I'd never met him before and was surprised by the man who greeted me early that morning – with his wavy grey hair falling upon a bohemian, open-collared white shirt he hardly appeared an overt rugger-bugger.

Taking a seat in the corner of the open-plan office, I explained to Dawie that I'd come to learn more of rugby in the Winelands and its great figures. He responded by telling me to be ready to take notes – he was all set to deliver a rugby lecture and I was more than happy to play the student.

'There are two influential figures you cannot escape in Stellenbosh rugby – Mr Markötter, or Mark, and Doc Craven,' he began. 'Mark covered roughly the first 50 years of rugby here and Craven covered the second 50.'

Markötter had a powerful influence on South African rugby. He was to a large extent the man behind the launch of rugby football in South Africa, certainly a man who did a great deal to boost it to its prominence, though his achievement would only be realised in others.

August Frederich Markötter was precocious enough to be called 'Oubaas' from an early age, and it showed.[33] Before his 15th birthday he was packed off to Victoria College, and it was there, in 1893, when rugby football had been played in South Africa for only 15 years, he first came into contact with the game. He fell in love with it straight away and wrote home to his parents on their mission station back in the Eastern Cape, asking their permission to play the game. 'If you do not give me permission,' he wrote, 'I shall play without it and I would hate to do that.'

Markötter would go on to captain Western Province Country

---

[33] Oubaas (Old Boss).

when they beat the British Isles 13-7 in 1903 and coach Stellenbosch from 1903 to 1956 (as well as working as a national selector from 1921 to 1938).[34]

Back then South Africa was a poor country trying to recover from the ravages of the Anglo-Boer Wars, but Oubaas spread his rugby gospel regardless. During his days at Stellenbosch, 53 Maties became Springboks, 130 played for Western Province, and Stellenbosch became the biggest rugby club in the world, as it still is. It was his first love. Well, just about. He once said, 'South Africa first, Stellenbosch second and Western Province a poor third.'

He was a clever selector and tactician. After the Lions of 1938 had lost the first two Tests in Cape Town they set sail for Port Elizabeth. Markötter was on the same ship. Disconsolate, the Lions asked him what they should do. He told them who to pick and what to do. They won the third Test!

Many of his most famous sayings were the result of too much drink, and he felt nothing of laying into players with his boot or shooting stick; but he could also end a stern talking-to with a soft word, cry at a funeral and send a bowl of fruit to a player in hospital. Craven maintained that Markötter suffered from an inferiority complex, hence his gruff exterior and reluctance to praise (and his excessive use of alcohol). Maybe he was just a romantic.[35]

Markötter took one look at his disciple, Craven, at a practice in 1929 and said, 'I'm keeping this one for South Africa.'

Danie Craven played for and captained the Springboks when they were at their best in the 1930s – leading the Boks to their

43

---

[34] There was no Boland in the early days and WP Country was distinct from WP Town. WP Town consisted of clubs in the Peninsula – Villagers, Hammies, Gardens, SACS, Bishops, et cetera. WP Country was chosen from Stellenbosch, Paarl, Wellington, Worcester, Malmesbury and so on. Markötter played for Stellenbosch until he tore ligaments in his knee playing cricket (soon after the historic win against the British Isles), then a career-ending injury.

[35] The research on Oubaas Markötter is indebted to the work of Paul Dobson.

first series victory in New Zealand (something savoured by precious few South African teams over the years).[36] Though most accomplished as a scrum half, Craven played at centre, fly half, fullback and eighth man on Springbok tours.[37] He later became a national selector and managed and coached the Springboks before becoming the president of the South African Rugby Board in 1956. At the time of his death in 1993 (in his beloved Stellenbosch), he was the executive president of SARFU.[38] As much of Dawie Snyman's time at Stellenbosch – as both a player and a coach – overlapped with Craven's, he had more insight than most into South Africa's most influential man in rugby.

'Mark and Doc,' Dawie said, 'took the elements of tradition, ethos, values, history and spirituality, and imparted these to the Stellenbosch students over a period of a hundred years. Only when something becomes a part of you can you reproduce it.'

Then it all got rather philosophical and in between making convoluted sketches and diagrams, he started throwing out questions like 'Who would you rather select: the one scoring the tries or the one creating the opportunities?' and 'What is our value system in life?'

'I'll tell you the facts of life,' Dawie finally said, coming to the end of his questioning and peering at me through his glasses that now sat low upon his nose. 'Firstly, no one has equal opportunities despite the fact that we try to create those equal opportunities. The second fact is professionalism: we are battling because of the

---

[36] The Springboks and All Blacks had met twice prior to this series – drawing both the 1921 and 1928 series. The All Blacks had never lost a series at home, the Springboks had not lost a series since 1896, and this series was billed as a world-title contest.

[37] Craven was primarily a scrum half though not, as is often believed, the inventor of the dive pass, although he developed it.

[38] That the Springboks played at all from the late 1960s on was probably due in the main to the personality and efforts of Danie Craven. It was also Doc Craven (three doctorates, it should be said, and an honoury one for good measure) and Louis Luyt who led a SARB delegation to Zimbabwe to meet with the exiled African National Congress in Harare.

way in which we manage professionalism in rugby.'

After a pause, Dawie asked me, 'What is the investment?'

At this point it really did feel like a return to my student days because I was struggling to connect the dots. Responding to the awkward silence, Dawie began to explain using the example of an apple farmer investing in his first fruits and future.

Right. The penny slowly began to drop. We were talking transformation and grassroots rugby. Both Markötter and Craven had ploughed their time into the future Springboks and the game's young souls.

'We would say our rugby is healthy because we've won two World Cups, but I don't think that necessarily proves the game is healthy here,' Dawie continued. 'We should be winning every World Cup! When I look at the talent when Paul Roos played Rondebosch Boys' the other day, or the games at Craven Week, I realise that our talent is unmatched.'

Paul Roos Gimnasium has produced more Springboks than any other school in South Africa. Bishops may be second on the log and have given the green jerseys to the national side, but an old boy of the Stellenbosch school conjured up that hallowed name for our national rugby team and subsequently the team emblem. Paul Roos, whilst captaining South Africa on their first overseas rugby tour in 1906-07, took the initiative and coined the tourists the 'Springbokken' before the local press could adopt a more unpleasant name – the tour, after all, had been organised four short years after the end of the second Boer War. In order to unite a culturally and linguistically divided side the bearded Roos also created the first Bok haka. The amusing 1928 photo of Phil Mostert's men – practicing their steps with all the awkwardness of those involved in a grade one play – is often thought of as our first rather bashful attempt to rival the All Blacks pre-match jig (though in actual fact it came before the Kiwi's adoption of the Maori war dance). Upon the deck of the *SS Gascon* en route to Southampton, Roos had his men learning what he described as a

'Hottentot hunting song'. However, it seemed to work, and the rugby the team played was regarded highly by the locals. Indeed, they were the only side to have defeated the great Welsh team of the early twentieth century.

Dawie continued to speak at length, moving effortlessly from stories of babysitting Hansie Cronje to talking about Dagbreek and Koshuis rugby, regularly referring to Craven throughout – it was the old doc who had brought him to WP to 'heal rifts' and take up the first Director of Coaching job there. However, the morning was wearing on and I had to bid farewell to Dawie, happy to have learnt a bit more about Paul, Mark and Doc, three wise men, all deeply rooted in South Africa's rugby history.

My journey to the East would continue via the world's longest wine route, Route 62. And by the end of a sobering and tedious trip through valleys of orchards and vineyards – Africa's not for sissies – there would even be some rugby to fill the empty wine glass.

Oudsthoorn and ostrich steaks were on the menu for the end of May, exactly a year from the anticipated Lions tour.

DIE STEM

Upon the scarlet Welsh rugby jerseys are the Prince of Wales feathers. These feathers have a long and distinguished history in heraldry, but their global boom began in Oudtshoorn in 1875. Fashionable feathers that could be produced with minimal effort for maximum gain transformed the fortunes of the farming district overnight. Like the gold rush 25 years before, immigrants arrived in droves as Oudtshoorn became the richest district in the vast Cape Colony.[39]

Today, Oudtshoorn also boasts some fine rugby. The biggest rugby day on the calender is Struisiesdag. Not suprisingly, it is between two schools: Oudtshoorn High School – nicknamed 'Stuisies' after volstruis (ostrich) – and Outeniqua High School (from neighbouring George) – nicknamed 'Kwaggas'.

The gentle community is stirred whenever the big brother from George arrives. The great fly half Hansie Brewis hailed from Oudtshoorn (he played for the Boks from 1949-53) as did Barry Wolmarans, of more recent Bok vintage. Wolmarans still has fond memories of the diminishing class time in the week leading up to Struisiesdag, to make space for the essential sing-song practices and additional rugby training. He once broke his arm in a match, and by Monday it was sitting in plaster. However, the crucial derby was arriving that very Saturday and his injury would surely end any chance of playing, so, during the week, he remained at home, informing his coach that he was merely a bit under the weather. By Thursday he had removed the plaster with his mother's scissors and pitched up for practice that afternoon. He was picked for the team and played the Saturday game, albeit with his arm still broken.

For culture vultures descending upon Oudtshoorn there is the Klein Karoo Nasionale Kunstefees, the first Afrikaans national arts festival. Those inclined to prioritise their budget around biltong and SuperSport are perhaps unlikely to diarise festivals and visit museums, but the Arbeidsgenot (translated 'The pleasure of work' which itself requires translation) Museum in

47

---

[39] 1,500 Jews (who comprised 90 per cent of the feather merchants) settled in the area, so that it became known as 'Little Jerusalem'. Ostriches became smuggled contraband to London, Paris and New York, and the penalty carried two years' jail time (with hard labour). Only in 1993 was a free market system introduced.

Oudtshoorn ought to be compulsory for all faithful rugger patriots, for that is the former home of Cornelis Jacobus Langenhoven. To most souties I'm sure this name has little relevance, but if your father-in-law happens to be a proud Afrikaner, then this is the name you may want to casually throw into conversation.

Langenhoven is revered by many Afrikaners because he championed Afrikaans language and identity, but he's best known for writing some of what South Africans sing before a rugby Test: 'Die Stem'.[40] Originally only three verses (but soon expanded to include 'God') today it is only the first verse that is belted out in 'Nkosi Sikelel' iAfrika'.[41]

Tour the museum and you'll find Langenhoven's bed, which a ship captain had unloaded after mistaking 'Mossel Bay' for 'Bombay', and the rooms where he entertained enemies and dominees. But he preferred entertaining the ordinary man in the street with his 50 books, of which most were fiction. Harry, the imaginary elephant, was his most infamous character, and a boulder outside Oudtshoorn that was inscribed with the name Harry ('Herrie') has since been declared a national monument.

He may have been the political jester of his time, but the fools were usually on the receiving end of his witty tongue. On one occasion in the Volksraad (House of Assembly), Langenhoven referred to half of the house as apes. When asked to recant, he replied: 'Mr Speaker, I withdraw my comments. Half of the house are not apes.'[42]

[40] 'Die Stem' was the South African national anthem from 1957 to 1994.

[41] Langenhoven's first verse of 'Die Stem' (The Call of South Africa) 1918:
   Uit die blou van onse hemel (Ringing out from our blue heavens)
   Uit die diepte van ons see (From our deep seas breaking round)
   Oor ons ewige gebergtes (Over everlasting mountains)
   Waar die kranse antwoord gee (Where the echoing crags resound)
Enoch Sontonga composed 'Nkosi Sikele' iAfrika' in 1897. The original version of 'Die Stem' is preserved in Stellebosch.

[42] Some accounts use 'donkeys'.

FROM GEORGE TO ELIZABETH

From the dusty Klein Karoo, I made my way toward the coast by way of the pass that snakes through the Outeniqua Mountains. A few hours later I arrived in the industrial centre of the busy Garden Route. George is home to the South Western District Eagles, the first smaller union on my journey. I took the opportunity to meet some of the 'rugby missionaries' growing the game's grassroots in the local community. I met a man from Belfast, the land of Willie John McBride, who had emigrated to George to work among Aids orphans, as well as other missionaries affiliated to churches, schools and foundations (even some from the union itself). Numerous programmes and initiatives were in the process of being implemented, although it was clear that this was the beginning of the smaller coastal unions that struggle to exist in the modern climate. Compared to the Big Five unions, those you find from George to East London have minimal resources and business acumen, and as the game grows ever more professional the gap only increases, with these unions doomed to be no more than feeders or fodder for their big brothers. Baba, a development officer at SWD, took me on a 'tour' of their small stadium and their facilities, though it ended a few minutes later at the union's mini-mobile gym on the B field. Baba seized the opportunity to impress me with some bench presses – my cue to push on.

An hour outside of the drier climes of Port Elizabeth is the surfing Mecca of Jeffreys Bay. For more than 40 years its legendary right-hand point break has lured surfers from around the world – mostly in midwinter – to brave the chilly waters and icy winds. When those rare giant swells arrive from the Atlantic and wrap themselves around Cape Point, they aim their sweeping energy along the reefs of South Africa's southern and eastern coast. When it's big enough, the J-Bay aqua artists can effortlessly glide along a single wave over all the multiple reefs that help make up the wave collectively known as 'Supertubes'. But for all its laid-back Eastern Cape charm, Jeffreys Bay doesn't *feel* like a surfer's paradise. It was once a rustic town established for a single wave, but those days are long gone. Now, surfing factory shops line its bland streets, doing their best to tempt anyone and everyone into parting with their money. A sport that once prided itself upon its distinctiveness and nonconformity has become increasingly overrun by big business. Perhaps it is inevitable that all sport eventually becomes about money. Perhaps it is the case with rugby too. We see it in the language that is used – teams are now 'brands' and players are 'assets'. We even see it at the grassroots, where parents auction off their children to the highest bidding union or academy and schools' sports directors hunt down and compete for the next crop of talented 13-year-olds armed with bursaries and scholarships. And yet, despite its challenges, I would argue that the pure form of the game remains addictively elegant and beautifully violent enough to encourage and grow a multitude of men and women who play and watch it for the simple joy that it brings.

South Africa's grassroots speak of a healthy future, and Grey High School is rugby's flagship in Port Elizabeth. Centrally placed along the Eastern Cape coast, the light blue blazers of Grey High travel *East* every year to the great Border schools and *North* into the nearby Klein Karoo to play Gill College, the old foe. It used to be that teams would also challenge farming-stock sides riddled with Jordaans, Schoemans, Coetzers, Marais, Schoombees and other well-known names from that district, but these days The Grey are prone to travel even further north, arriving at their near namesake, Grey College. For years, Grey College have been the strongest school in schools rugby, and this game is the one most Grey High teams build their season upon. There is also a trip *West* to Cape Town, most recently to play Wynberg – these are, after all, the days when schools prefer to grow derbies with one another based on whether their opponents can offer all their sides a Saturday game, and it is inevitable that the schools which can field over 20 teams any given weekend are consistently strong and enjoy a surplus of good depth with each new year.

Despite its healthy performances today, Grey High's rugby birth was anything but glamorous. Some kind of football was played on the rough ground of the Donkin Reserve in front of the Institute building in the early days. We know this because the story of the rector being 'dumped' – in the true sense of the rugby jargon – has lived on until the present day. Soon after arriving at The Grey in 1863, Rector Reverend Johnson joined an informal game (of some rugger version) and was promptly flattened by one of the senior boys. He pronounced rugby 'a very rough game' but had the good grace not to ban it. However, rugby still wasn't taken very seriously, with the school magazine telling us that the boys practiced in 'straw hats and black coats'. The biggest problem, as reported in the school magazine in 1895, was 'the lack of rivalry which would prove strong enough to develop excellence'. And, painfully, by 1905 the magazine's football report covered only soccer.

Despite plunging to these sacrilegious sporting depths rugby would soon take its rightful place; the antidote, of course, delivered through rugby people. For most Eastern Cape schools, the revival began in the 1920s when schools grew in number and the great rivalries were born – via ox cart and involving many a numb backside. At Grey, Rector Way was one of the men who made a difference. His passion for the game was such that he once called one S. B. Bowker, a boarder from Bathurst, to his offices on a Monday morning and criticised him for getting 'bottled up' on the wing in two pointless draws against St Andrew's.

That Saturday, Bowker switched places with the fly half during one passage of play and then tore down the middle of the field to deposit the ball under the poles for the winning points in a tightly contested game. When the Rector next saw him, he said, 'Bowker, take this.' It was a 10-bob note.

The Grey's first matches were played at venues in St George's Park. Typically Victorian, Rector Way was so protective of his precious cricket pitch that even after the move to Mill Park from the Institute building near the centre of the city, rugby continued to be played mostly on the local grounds of the Crusader Club. However, rugby players may have had cause to be grateful that they had to travel to play home matches as one of Mr Way's unique recipes for pitch preparation on the Front Field under the Clock Tower was ox blood.

The early dabblings with soccer forgotten, the school soon enjoyed remarkable success. The 1923 u16A team boasted a record few could ever match:

Points for: 431
Points against: 0

Some even appreciated their rugby so much that they never seemed to leave. This seemed especially true of bearded front rankers, who did not excel academically and were seemingly happy to fail standard nine as it gave them another year in the first rugby team. Of course, this practice was as rife amongst other schools – especially in the 1960s and 70s, when it was noted that some 'boys' were celebrating 21st birthdays whilst still at school.[43]

But perhaps the finest Grey High anecdote I have heard was

---

[43] At the time private schools were inclined to fill their post-matric classes with 'boys' that would bolster their rugby sides. This 'tradition' has been thrown out in recent years to the dismay of countless front rankers and their families.

that involving the great Alan Read, who was later to play for Western Province and the Junior Springboks. During the 1965 season he was practicing his penalty kicks with his bare feet from the halfway line of the Pyott field. His great mate, Jon Green, who was standing under the far poles, yelled to him that he did not have 'a hope in hell in putting the kick over'. Read then launched a kick but the ball sailed just short, smacking the bar directly. The bar was not secure. It bounced off the mounting and fell upon Green's head. A prone Green was carted off to sick bay, and later hospital, but the gathered onlookers all thought it quite a joke at the time.

It is the memories and experiences of the school years that have many old boys sending their sons to their alma mater. Familiar names like Dakin, Bennett and Miller are fourth-generation-old Greys, all undergoing the self-same initiations as their great-grandfathers before them. Well, just about.

III

THE EASTERN CAPE

St Andrew's

July 2008

THE JERSEY TROPHIES

Despite remaining a largely underdeveloped region, the Eastern Cape can boast of a rich rugby heritage and an established following for the game. The area has always been the stronghold of black rugby in South Africa, and my first port of call would be in the heart of a township, where I was to meet an influential rugby man – a white man, to be unpolitically correct.

I waited for Theo Pieterse at a derelict New Brighton petrol station just beyond gusty Port Elizabeth. When he finally arrived, the blond Afrikaner led me through the township and on to Dan Qeqe Stadium. Theo played some good rugby in his day, alongside Hannes Marais and Gavin Cowley for Port Elizabeth University, before taking up a teaching position at Itembilihle. That was three decades ago.

A tournament was on the go when we arrived – the semi-finals in progress – and Theo's side, Itembilihle, were the hot favourites to take the trophy. We made our way across to the dusty fields, the animated Theo greeting familiar rugby faces in a mix of English, fluent Xhosa and Afrikaans.

'Ja, I'm the Dutchman of the Township,' he said, smiling at my reaction to his linguistic dexterity. 'But the boys call me "Umlungu", which is a respectful term for a white bloke.'

Since his arrival at the school in 1979, Theo has transformed a school obsessed with soccer into a rugby powerhouse. They can boast of more than a few established rugby school scalps (an array of glittering cups stand proudly in the school's trophy cabinet), and all this despite the fact that they lack the most basic finances to fund first aid, transport or maintenance of a home rugby field. In addition to which Theo usually has to feed the 15 hungry bellies before any warm-up or game takes place. Not quite the difficulties faced by most rugby-playing schools.

The game itself looked like a spirited contest. The pace was frenetic and the handling skills were as fine as you would see in any schools rugby game – the ball being passed with purpose and intent. While we watched from the touchline Theo introduced me to Shorty, the 15-year-old team manager, telling me that his job was 'to carry the kicking tee and pick up teeth'.

The game ended in yet another victory for the local lads. Not all were overjoyed though, especially their burly hooker. 'He's not a happy chappy,' Theo murmured to me. 'He'll be playing the final soon, his third game of the day, and he still hasn't eaten a real meal.'

Well, not quite, because the finals never actually happened. Itembilihle took to the field, full of confidence and vigour. About 20 minutes later the opposition arrived. And about 10 minutes after that, the ref, ready to blow his fourth game in a row. But not all camps were happy. The opponents were short of players and those present were unwilling to take on a side that played a hard game on an even harder field. Within the first minute a boy lay injured and they urged the ref to call off the game. The overweight ref, already wheezing, was happy to oblige.

'Oh, jeez,' Theo grumbled. 'Now you see the disorganisation here. Always so unpredictable.'

The anticlimax, however, did not deprive the boys of their coveted trophies at the prize-giving: jerseys, socks and shorts. And rarely have I seen boys with wider smiles than when they received their new rugby jerseys.

The spirit of South African rugby is alive and well if men like Theo Pieterse and others are ploughing their time and effort into developing what will undoubtedly prove to be the next generation of Springboks. Their work shows up overnight initiatives and quick financial 'fixes', where money is pumped into superficial transformation, but where precious little is done about developing the raw talent so ready and keen to be coached.

Itembilihle means 'good hope' and perhaps, with men like Pieterse and his fellow teachers around, there is indeed a hopeful future.

THE FORGOTTEN

From PE, I headed north for Route 63, free from concrete and clamour, and into the heart of South Africa. There is something hauntingly beautiful about this vast frontier country. It's rugged and arid, and quite content to remain that way. To the casual tourist the placid platteland may seem like nothing more than a few dry, dusty old dorps locked away in some timeless land. Well, that wouldn't be completely inaccurate. But then it was their passionate rugby folk I was on my way to see, and I had heard that they were as rugby crazed as the mad Mooloo men of Waikato.

There's always an enthusiastic, if small attendance at a platteland club game. Squawking women, oupas (whose oupas watched before them) and half a dozen cows with care-free bowels are always sure to pitch up. And once the necessities are in place – the first-aid kit (a packet of melting ice) and the corrugated iron door of the long drop (that is easily detachable and often used as a stretcher) – the stage is set for the only rugby match that counts in the country.[44] Platteland rugby is also some of the most partisan. Be prepared to be on the receiving end of some spitting vitriol if you even think about trying to beat the local town, and that's just from the touch judge. Score a try on the day of the derby and you have etched your name into the hearts of the local poppies and your name will echo in the bar at the local Royal Hotel. Return years later and those grey wrinkled souls huddled around the bar will still be talking about the try you scored against 'Brakfonteinspruit'.

Somerset East was my first destination. Nestled between the Fish and the Kei Rivers, and with the Boschberg Mountains rising up behind it, this old settlement is the home to Gill College, a school founded in 1869 and which has had the Du Plessis brothers (Willie, Michael and Carel), among others, grace its fields.

The First XV field at Gill is named after C A Coppens, whose grave lies deep within the school grounds. He coached rugby at the school for 50 years, instructing the boys in old school traditions and disciplines. Part of that was neatness – even on the rugby field. During a first-team game in the early 1990s, Jaco Heyes wished to get on with his scrum-half duties and put the ball into the bound and waiting scrum. But he could not. The problem was *not* the old 'foot up' rule, or even the front rows pushing too early. It was his hooker's socks. They were down, sitting untidily upon his bootlaces. Coppens would have turned

---

[44] Whether it is concussion or a broken ankle, there's nothing that ice and a swig of the linesman's beer won't fix in these parts. A bucket of sand for the kicker is also a 'modern novelty' and generally scoffed at. The kicker's left boot will more than suffice. Nor are portable mini whiteboards or blackboards, for that matter, required: the coach's scribbled tactics fit just fine on the back of a pack of cigarettes (which will be hastily stuffed in one of the captain's socks before kick-off).

in his grave, Jaco reasoned. And so, instead of putting the ball in, he dived beneath the front rows of the two restless packs and began pulling up his hooker's socks.

The small co-ed school at the foot of the Boschberg Mountains has always punched admirably above its weight, even with barely 100 boys. Though derbies against the big Border and PE schools no longer take place, it still travels far and wide to knock some schools down to size. And with the home derby comes the home support. By early Saturday morning, farmers have surrounded the field with their bakkies to sample some fine schools rugby.

But perhaps the finest grassroots rugby is being played on a farm outside nearby Cradock.

PLAASLEWE

Marlow is the premier rugby school of the North Eastern Cape, and its First XV regularly ranks among the country's finest – not bad for a small agricultural school known among its own as 'Wolram'. Their six buses travel some 35,000 kilometres each year seeking out opposition as far afield as Bloemfontein and Kimberley. When one spends many a long hour in a bakkie on a dusty road, stories are sure to abound. I'd heard a good few, many revolving around a Marlow old boy or teacher, with the occasional bottle of some toxic concoction thrown in for good measure ...

Cradock is not the most central of places and anyone there

who wished to watch a big rugby game would have to travel through to PE. One year, a number of Marlow boys and teachers had travelled to the coastal city to watch the mighty All Blacks play against Eastern Province at the Boet Erasmus (in those years, EP boasted a fine fly half and kicker by the name of Gordon Jordaan). As people gathered about the gates waiting to enter through the turnstiles a Salvation Army preacher boldly proclaimed the Gospel to those queuing. 'Who will save you on this day?' he repeatedly bellowed with passion and gusto. Nearby stood a wobbly spectator, who had enjoyed a few drinks already. Again, the preacher shouted to the masses, 'Who will save you on this day?' The drunkard took it upon himself to slur an answer: 'Moenie worry nie, man! Gordon Jordaan *shal* dit doen!'

On another occasion, Marlow teacher Anton Anthony and some others had caught a lift with a Roman Catholic priest to the Baai (PE), where a big game was due to be played. The Windy City was bitterly cold that wintry evening, and by the time the priest had come to collect them after the game, they had all had a number of nips of sherry to fight off the bone-chilling conditions. While they were initially in a merry mood on their way back to Cradock, it wasn't long before the boys all began to develop a desperate thirst due to the alcohol they had consumed. The priest had no water in the car, so when the distant glimmer of a river was seen by one of the Marlow party, they begged him to stop. Pulling over, the priest watched as the Marlow men clambered out and attempted to navigate the steep bank beside the road on unsteady legs. Eventually, they arrived at the sparkling source. But all was not quite as it seemed. 'Father, it's frozen!' the first disappointed bloke hollered back. The priest got out of the vehicle, surveyed the shining surface below, and informed his disillusioned companions that a quenching pot of gold was not to be found at the end of their rainbow. Instead, they had stumbled across the shiny, freshly laid surface of a tarred road.

In its younger days, Marlow was a humble community and the

only land on the farm even vaguely flat enough to accommodate some rugby was between the rail tracks and hay shed. However, despite the thick Karoo bush and the protruding rocks, the enthusiasm for the game of rugby kept boiling over, and for 15 years this patch of rough, uncultivated land was the site of much tackling and scrumming. Eventually, the Marlow Rugby Club was founded and by the mid-1980s, Marlow had 180 boys, *all* of whom played rugby.[45] Except for one bloke, according to Bok Willie Meyer, who had a wooden leg. However, this did not deter him from regularly joining his mates for touch rugby.

When the end of school holidays means a return to the confines of a boarding house on an isolated farm, you are bound to make lasting friendships. Referee André Watson once enjoyed a first-hand experience of this. In 1998, while refereeing a competitive match between Border and the Free State Cheetahs in Bloemfontein, a line-out had been formed late in the second half. As the ball was about to be thrown in, Cheetahs prop Willie Meyer stepped across the line-out and grabbed the private parts of Border lock Streicher Botha. As he did so, Meyer called across to Watson: 'Wattie, tell this man: my ball is my ball and his ball is *also* my ball.' Watson was completely unprepared for this, and even less well prepared for the response of Streicher, who doubled over laughing and could not even jump in the line-out when play resumed. Watson later learnt that Meyer and Streicher were good mates from their days at Marlow, though that is not to say this is a common 'Wolram welkom'.[46]

Although the Western Cape may boast of older bricks and mortar, the clubs and schools that were established in the Eastern Cape hold a special place in the history of South African rugby. It was not difficult for rugby to find a home in the rural communities here. The land here grew tough farmers' sons who were inclined

[45] Marlow Rugby Club was founded in 1932 after a meeting in the school's classroom.

[46] The story was captured in *André Watson: The Autobiography*.

to a tough game. Numerous Springboks have subsequently learnt their rugby on the dry Eastern Cape veld, and although these days most schools and clubs are struggling to exist, a sprightly rugby spirit remains deeply embedded in this part of South Africa.

I would be staying a few nights on a game farm in nearby Adelaide, owned by Chris Bush, the son-in-law of artist Tony Grogan. There I would meet some of the locals, all farmers and all with rugby backgrounds, who would shed some light on the unique rugby of the platteland.

Every good rugby story from the platteland seems to begin or end at the hotel (and the pub therein). They are always at the epicentre of everything that happens in the town. Midgley's Hotel is on Adelaide's dusty town square. Just as these towns seem to exist in some kind of timeless 1960s vacuum, so to do their legends hail from the days of old. Have a drink in Midgley's and you're bound to hear the name of 'Baba Botha' a dozen times – 'A player more cheeky than Ricky Januarie and as talented as Fourie!' I was told.

The local heroes seem far more entrenched in rugby folklore here than Francois Pienaar or John Smit could ever be, and though the stories are old, memories remain fresh. However, if the current trends continue it is unlikely that these great rugby battles of the past will be repeated. In 1989, 44 rugby clubs spanned the North Eastern Cape, from Cookhouse to Burgersdorp and Jansenville. At that time every town had its own rugby club, and could field at least two teams. They played in strong organised leagues, and welcomed 'friendlies' against touring sides. They were well-supported and were financially self-supporting. There were even regional teams – the Midlands, Karoo and the North East District. From these sides, a provincial team was selected, and occasionally it would also play touring international teams. There were at least 500 active club-rugby players in the platteland. The clubs were vibrant and their rugby healthy. Today, only four of those original clubs remain. Granted, most were traditionally 'white' clubs, and today 14 'black' and 'coloured' clubs exist, but even considering this it is clear that the face of rugby in this part of the country has changed dramatically in 20 short years. The days when a small technical school like Adelaide produced world-class rugby men like Os du Randt, Garry Pagel and Anton Leonard seem an increasingly distant memory.[47]

In the relatively short time that Chris Bush has owned Molweni, the 8,500 hectare game farm has grown in value to over 100 million rand.[48] Not too bad for a Kearnsey boy reared in the city. Hunting is what pays the farm's bills – well-heeled foreigners or South Africans come here regularly – but Chris is discerning when it comes to his clientele.

'I prefer to not invite your biltong bandits,' he told me as we made our way towards the thatched guest house. 'You know, the type that wake up hung-over on a Saturday morning and are keen to shoot the biggest horns they can find. We have trackers and our own guys accompanying the hunters to ensure it's all done above board. Trophies can be taken home but the meat remains on the farm so that it can be used.'

As I dumped my bags in the guest cottage, Chris told me that two berg winds had been driving fires along the Amatola and Winterberg Mountains the whole day. He was understandably concerned and our conversation was regularly interrupted by calls updating him on the direction the fires were taking. Talk of the fires also dominated the initial exchanges as Julian Bennett –

---

[47] Craven Week, where so much of the finest young talent bursts upon the scene, has seen a shifting and unsettled balance for a number of decades. The number of teams, what they are called and how many development, country and international sides are in attendance has changed on an annual basis. By the turn of the century, the 30 sides and 660 players that used to attend Craven Week had been pruned to 16 South African teams and 352 players. Someone had to lose out and it would, of course, be the smaller unions. The North Eastern Cape, which provided 20 players to Craven Week in 1996, supplied none in 2005 – though sanity prevailed when Craven Week later opened its doors again to the talented boys of these areas.

[48] Molweni is a communal Xhosa greeting.

a fine rugby player in his day and the father of Springbok Russell Bennett – and Antonie Lombard – who farmed cattle and sheep nearby, and whose father had also played for the Boks – pulled up their dusty bakkies outside the main house as the early evening sun began to set. It wasn't long before a few others also arrived, including the reserved Garry Pagel. Though they all farmed 'nearby', some had driven up to an hour on dirt roads to reach the informal gathering and they could be forgiven for being a little late.

We sat on the stoep to a spread of dried meats, snacks and drinks. As we awaited a few more arrivals, I began to hear the stories of men whose families had long ago put down roots in the heart of this land. Glance at any school history book today and you'd swear that Isandlwana and Rorke's Drift were the only battles in South African history, but the fascinating Frontier Wars are worth hearing about. When plains were wide and sparsely inhabited, a few migrating Boers travelled into lands settled by the Khoi (who did not wish them to be there) and Xhosa (who were encroaching from the east). The land offered pasture for their livestock, abundant fresh water and a new beginning. When land became disputed, the Boers looked to the local director of the Dutch East India Company, Van Plettenberg, who arranged for them to be escorted to the nearest Xhosa kraal. This belonged to a chieftain named Koba, who can be identified as a son of Titi, then ruler of the amaGwali Xhosa.[49] The governor bartered with Koba and eventually brokered a deal in which the land was divided on either side of the Fish River – Van Plettenberg claiming all of the land west of the Fish River for the Dutch, even that already occupied by five Xhosa tribes. An armed commando made sure the instructions were adhered to and the inevitable blood was spilt and livestock stolen. It would be the opening salvo in the

---

[49] Here, one of the party created a small sensation when he produced a mirror and showed the Xhosa their reflections. One maiden, the diarist records, was so entranced that she bared her breasts and made them bob and jump in the reflecting glass.

first war on the Eastern Cape frontier.[50]

When the dust settled the colonists began to put down roots, and it wasn't long before schools were established. Healthy rugby clubs emerged in the late 1800s as the sport grew in popularity. However, playing in a country league involved travelling great distances – often by wagon. Even within living memory the actual mechanics of running a league in this immense landscape boggle the mind – Antonie recalled travelling for eight hours on horseback to arrive at a game in Cradock.

As night fell I began to listen to stories of what was and what is; of how South African rugby is doing in these forgotten areas. Doc Craven once said that great players were born and bred in the rural areas where they developed both physical coordination and confidence in their abilities. However, the decline of rugby in the Eastern Cape platteland had been inexorable since the early 70s; the issues deep-set, perhaps even insurmountable.

Just beyond Port Elizabeth, on a small hill off the N2 highway, stands an old Methodist missionary church where my great-grandfather once ministered. It is here that the road forks: the N2 continuing inland to Grahamstown while the Sunshine Coast road leads to Port Alfred and East London. I took a left, heading north with the fiery platteland sunset behind me, onward to a town that lies in the heart of this frontier country.

---

[50] Details of the Boer expansion into the Eastern Cape, and the subsequent wars, is best read in John Milton, *The Edges of War: A History of the Frontier Wars 1702-1878.*

SAINTS AND SCHOLARS

Grahamstown may now be revered for its churches and university, but it was founded as a frontier town in 1819 (at a time when Britain was trying to wrest land and power from the Xhosa). Settlers arrived from 1820 onwards, many of whom were Methodists, and with them came the game of rugby football. There was an understanding in those days that rugby was important to a boy's welfare. This derived from grand notions of muscular Christianity and healthy ambition. Thomas Hughes, the best-selling author of *Tom Brown's Schooldays*, the book which spurred on early rugby growth, wrote:

> Far say, you don't see much in it at all, nothing bar a smuggling mass of boys, and a leather ball, which seems to excite them all to a great fury as a red rag to a bull [...] a battle would look much the same to you, except that the boys would be men and the balls iron.[51]

At St Andrew's College, sport became compulsory and every pupil was to attend two rugby practices a week. In fact, only recently was there an alternative winter sporting option (hockey) to rugby. However, unlike in Britain, where rugby was taught almost exclusively in public schools and was seen as a game for the upper classes, the game did move fairly freely between the races (let alone the class groups) and by the late 1800s there were numerous clubs catering for the needs of almost every racial group. In the Eastern Cape, missionaries established churches and schools, and with them, organised sport. Soon, young Xhosa men were taking a liking to rugby, something which is still the

---

[51] Thomas Hughes, *Rugby and Football*.

case in the country's south-east.[52]

St Andrew's have enjoyed numerous renowned coaches over the years, but perhaps the most famous is Danie Craven himself. Already a national hero and in the prime of his sporting career, Craven took up a job as teacher of English and Afrikaans at St Andrew's in 1936 (later becoming a tutor in Upper House and coach of the u16s). Despite his heavy workload, as well as all the attention he received when practicing his rugby or his swimming in his spare time, he went on to be selected as vice captain of the 1937 Springbok side to tour New Zealand and Australia.[53]

The St Andrew's First XV rugby jersey has alternating eight-inch stripes of light and dark blue. It was first introduced in 1904, and the other trappings of the English public school weren't far behind: long socks, blazers and caps and scarves.[54]

In his will of 1903, Cecil John Rhodes established 20 annual colonial scholarships which were distributed to young men across the Commonwealth. He included St Andrew's as one of the four South African schools that could annually award such a scholarship. The other schools were the South African College Schools (SACS), Victoria College (now Paul Roos Gimnasium) and the Diocesan College (Bishops).[55]

---

[52] The Reverend Robert John Mullins first aroused Xhosa interest in the game at an institute for Xhosa speakers attached to St Andrew's, which started in 1859.

[53] As already mentioned, this team, which included old Andrean D. van der Vywer, went on to beat Australia 2-0, and New Zealand 2-1 – in the process becoming the first and only Springbok side to have ever won a Test series against New Zealand in New Zealand.

[54] Rugby School adopted football dress in the 1830s. Soon long white pants and coloured caps and jerseys to distinguish teams had become the norm.

[55] By 1907 St Andrew's had produced five Rhodes Scholars at Oxford. The following is a report on the Oxford inter-varsity match from *The Sportsman*: 'The real success of the Oxford team were their halves, both of which hailing from St Andrew's College in South Africa. No fewer than half a dozen of the Oxford XV hail from South Africa, including the two half backs, five of the six having been educated at St Andrew's College. It must be a source of great satisfaction to South African footballers, that a young colonial college should turn out such clever recruits for English Universities. Our English Public Schools must look to their laurels.'

As schools grew and flourished, so too did their rugby. While one of the oldest school derbies in South Africa is between St Andrew's and Graeme College, and the traditional game is against Bishops of Cape Town, the game that awakens slumbersome Grahamstown is K-Day, the local derby between Saints and Kingswood.[56] Unlike the game that would be played in Cape Town, this derby takes a full day to wind up, culminating in the First XV kick-off in the late afternoon. In 1896, St Andrew's shrewdly began this long rivalry when Kingswood was still a soccer school. But it all got serious a decade later, and today K-Day is all-important, as one story reveals.

In 1964, St Andrew's was enjoying a successful rugby season. Eric Norton was the hard-as-nails coach at the time, a rugby legend who coached possibly the greatest decade of rugby yet seen at the school (the 1950s). In those days, prefects were permitted to smoke at College but the First XV had entered into a gentleman's agreement with Norton that no member would smoke except after the game on the Saturday night. At about 10pm, on the eve of the Kingswood match, Norton knocked on the Upper House study door of No. 8 and captain D. J. Comyn. He informed the captain that he had just seen Dish Pringle, the team's best line-out forward, smoking in the Graham House prefects' common room. 'I'm going to drop him for the game,' Norton said. 'We had a gentleman's agreement.'

The team was depleted as it was and much of their strategy depended on the line-out – the training in the week had been spent perfecting it with Dish. But the coach was adamant. With no room for negotiation, Comyn stood up and opened the top drawer of his chest. He picked out his colours badge and declared: 'If you drop Pringle, you drop me.'

Norton turned on his heel and left Comyn to a sleepless night.

---

[56] Apparently the first game between these two sides took place on 13 April 1878. Graeme won by a try to a goal. *Grocott's Penny Mail* officially records a game on 10 September 1886.

In the end neither of the boys were dropped for the game, and both went on to play grand roles as St Andrew's beat Kingswood 5-0.

Staunch support arrives every K-Day; parents and professionals, working-class men and labourers. Black support has always been prominent, as old Andrean Nick Mallett once discovered after the Kingswood clash. An elated black man came running over to him and revealed two hands full of coins and notes. 'Take some! Take some!' the overjoyed man cried. Mallett was moved but refused the man's winnings.

A few weeks earlier I had briefly broken my journey east to return to Cape Town and attend the launch of a book I had co-authored. The launch was to be screened live on the weekly rugby programme, *Boots & All*, but it was also my chance to meet with Mallett, who was in the country with the Italian side ahead of their Test against the Boks at Newlands.

Unfortunately, despite my finest endeavours – pestering staff in hotel lobbies and leaving messages on the voicemail of numerous cellphones – Mallet remained elusive. In fact, it was only on the eve of the Test that I learnt that Mallett, that wandering rugby gypsy, was happy to meet with me at his hotel that evening (come Sunday morning he'd be on a flight to Buenos Aires for a Test against Argentina).

Mallett is a charismatic man, perfectly suited to working among the extroverted and passionate rugby folk of Italy and, previously, France. The Argentinians, French and Italians bring such emotion to a game originally the domain of the stiff upper lip that it's indeed a blessing to have some of them swap soccer V-necks for collared rugger jerseys. New Zealand legend John Kirwan was another foreigner who coached the *Azzurri*. Also blessed with more than his fair share of charisma, he once stated: 'I yell and scream like they do. I'm the worst of them. Totally. I'm a nightmare. Once they gave me the passport that was it – I started throwing my hands in the air, drinking red wine and flying off the handle.'

A generic trait common to all coaches, according to Fred Allen, is that 'they are seldom satisfied, seldom happy and seldom at home.'

This is probably because rugby coaches are arguably rugby's most passionate men. Many even give up the land of their birth to seek new challenges elsewhere and although these hardships are not without their financial reward, it is also important to consider that many of these coaches began their careers in schools rugby – hardly the most well-paid profession in the world. Eddie Jones, Graham Henry, Jake White, Frank Hadden, Brian Ashton and Nick Mallett are just the tip of the rugby teacher/ coach iceberg. Teachers are arguably the most influential rugby *missionaries* any country has, though when I put this to Mallett, he pondered if *mercenary* was not the word I sought.

Nick sat on a couch across from me in the hotel lounge. You could swear he would be playing the next day; clearly a hands-on rugby session had just finished as he sat sweating in rugby shorts, long socks and muddied boots. Ironically, the last time Italy arrived in South Africa, Mallett was the Bok coach. The dark-browed, broad-shouldered man has done much in the decade since growing a world-beating Bok team (and subsequently getting the boot for questioning the establishment's overzealous ticket pricing). His outspokenness has always stemmed from his individuality, and this was pretty evident from his early years in the country school of Peterhouse in Rhodesia. There, as a five-year-old, he created his finest Picasso, which delayed the opening of a new block of classrooms, he navigated his tricycle over puff adders and broke, on average, two pairs of reading glasses a week.

'As a laaitie at a school like that you're going to get up to mischief,' Nick said and smiled. 'But the 30 pairs of glasses I went through there ... It was all rather pointless. In the end they reckoned my eyesight was fine after all!'

It was perhaps because of his individualism that hostel life beckoned, but boarding as a primary-school lad in Cape Town was a 'hardening experience'.

'Boarding in a boys' school brings a lot of independence,' Nick began. 'Some people think it cultivates bad qualities. For instance, showing sympathy or admitting you are struggling in a boarding environment is often seen as weakness. It can almost be a *Lord of the Flies* psyche. But there are also positive aspects. All battles are *your* battles, and that certainly grows your confidence. I've had plenty of ups and downs in my sporting career, but it doesn't worry me as much as it may have worried others.'

After Mallet had completed his primary education, his father thought it better to send his son to boarding school in Grahamstown rather than move him to Bishops, where he had recently taken up the post of headmaster. It turned out to be a good decision. Nick excelled at St Andrew's College.

'If you played good sport, you quickly earned respect amongst your peers,' Nick explained. '"A healthy body leads to a healthy mind" was the mantra, though it was probably a weakness of many boarding schools then, where too much emphasis was placed upon sport. I don't think it's the case now; my son has gone through Bishops and it's a bit more balanced these days.'

Mallett has nothing but praise for his coaches at St Andrew's, but he worries about the current situation.

'In the 60s and 70s you had a good lifestyle if you were a teacher, and it was a popular profession for many,' he told me. 'But today, it's hardly an option for a personable young male who can offer something academically and on the sports field. To maintain the standards for a good school today requires hard financial decisions. Many old boys, who don't enjoy seeing standards dip, also recognise this and put some money back into their schools.'

It's always been a rich rugby education when I've met with Mallett. He sits on the edge of the couch, his eyes wide and glowing as he speaks about a game that has been central to his life. He speaks passionately about the great derbies of the country, some of which he's been fortunate enough to be a part of. He's adamant that South Africa's clubs should be privatised. Nor does he harbour any regrets over not rightfully inheriting the '97 team against the Lions after the sacking of Markgraaff. Perhaps his only regret (in true rugby spirit) is the misadministration of many with little rugby understanding or professional experience.

'We have a unique cultural group in South Africa – the Afrikaners,' Mallet said, touching on an issue close to his heart. 'Like the Samoans and islanders, they are ideally suited to the game of rugby. They have the necessary physical qualities; they're big and fast. Of course we need to develop all our cultural groups, but we need to be careful about how politically correct we try to be to the detriment of perhaps our greatest rugby asset: the young Afrikaner boy who has grown up wanting to represent the Boks. And growing the game also begins with ticket prices! The days of families attending a game together are long gone. And yet we still have half-empty stadiums even when the Boks pitch up. You can't directly blame the unions. They need to recoup the money they owe SA Rugby for hosting a Test. So they must do away with some of this so that the supporters don't indirectly fit an enormous bill.'

Nick Mallett is a journeyman – from coaching the Boks in 15 Tests against the great Tri-Nations foes, to playing and coaching careers in France (12 years) and Italy – but you get the sense that if more of his ilk were involved in the game, more rugby decisions would be made to the benefit of the game, and that its spirit would be closely guarded. For now, the Italian rugby renaissance is his priority. But he'll be back one day.

The first Methodist school in the country, the red-bricked Kingswood College, was established in Grahamstown and for over a century there's been a tense but healthy rugby rivalry between it and its Anglican neighbour. In 1911 St Andrew's were beaten 9-4 in a match in which Rhodes students had joined the Kingswood side to balance the participation of other Rhodes students who were living at St Andrew's and playing for their First XV. Following the match a heated debate sprang up – not too dissimilar to the ongoing post-matric rugby player argument today – and fixtures between the schools were subsequently suspended. They only resumed in 1918 – the year future Springboks Bennie Osler and Jack Slater would make up the Kingswood line-up. They beat St Andrew's twice that year and thrashed the Crusaders Rugby Club, from PE, 24-3.[57]

In 1928, South Africa played the All Blacks – the second ever series between the two nations who were hastily establishing rugby's greatest rivalry. The first Test of that series is known as the 'Kingswood Test', a game won 17-0 by the Boks, where all 17 points were scored by old Kingswoodians. Slater scored a try and Bennie Osler kicked the rest of the points.[58]

At the end of the game it was obvious to everyone that the Boks had unearthed a world-beating fly half – the freckled, fair-haired Bennie Osler. South Africa never lost an international series with him at fly half, Western Province kept the Currie Cup when he played at Newlands, and UCT, Hamiltons and Villagers all won the Grand Challenge as he moved from one club to another.

However, Osler's name is not only immortalised in rugby journals. It can also be found on the pews of the gallery of Kingswood Commemoration Church – where he carved it himself with his very own penknife. Scores of names fill the once empty

[57] Jack Slater's father was Josiah Slater, whose influence on Grahamstown remains in the form of *Grocott's Mail*, the oldest surviving independent newspaper in South Africa. It was founded in 1870 as *Grocott's Penny Mail*, but incorporated the *Grahamstown Journal* (the first edition of which was printed in 1831), of which Slater was the proprietor. Jack Slater played for the famous 1918 Kingswood First XV and the 1928 Springboks, and was the school's headmaster from 1955-64.

[58] Danie Craven, soon to be a St Andrew's teacher, was Osler's halfback partner that day.

woodwork, and the fact that many are duplicated upon the lists of those who fell in the World Wars adds a haunting beauty to what might otherwise be dismissed by visitors as vandalism.

As K-Day rugby grew, so too did its traditions. One such tradition now takes place in the dining hall on the eve of all matches. At the end of the meal, the rugby captain approaches the master in charge and asks his permission for the rugby war cry to be performed. Permission granted, a signal is given and the walls reverberate with the chanting of 'Sana Madoda'. On the eve of K-Day this tradition is taken to the next level as the entire school congregates on the circle in front of the main entrance to the school. Surrounding the First XV, the school are led in song and their war cries reverberate across town and down upon College. St Andrew's, of course, reciprocate and these chants go back and forth between the two schools, the townsfolk enjoying an entertaining and enthusiastic concert.

A WORLD CUP GIANT

76   I've arrived in East London to meet with one of the finest rugby locks in Springbok history. Locks are traditionally the jumpers in the team, though more recently that role has been increasingly poached by those who do their work in the back row. So the lock today tends to be the mug flapping his arms about in a line-out while the ball flies over him, or the bloke heaving away in the middle of a scrum watching the ball pass below his feet. This, of

course, is not always the case for professional locks. Beyond the expected requirements – in terms of height and physique – they also often boast additional skills almost unheard of in amateur second-rowers. They can run. They can pass. Sometimes they can even do both simultaneously (though this can result in a speed wobble). They also tend to get dressed up: many tape their thighs, wrists and arms, and wear headgear. I still prefer the old-school locks who wore tape around their ears. Mark Andrews was my favourite. With a gaping hole between his front teeth and a noticeable lack of hair he was no pretty-boy rugby player. What was endearing, however, was the cheeky schoolboy smile that appeared regularly. Whether it was because he was enjoying the banter or because he had committed another undetected crime, I was never sure.

I had arranged to meet with the great lock on the fields of our alma mater, Selborne College. For the sake of conjuring up the old stories, I've always enjoyed speaking to the past greats beside the fields upon which their rugby was moulded. Mark was waiting at the empty war memorial, the grandstand that looks down on the main rugby field and the school beyond it. Although the school was still on holiday and the campus was eerily quiet, I'm sure Mark was reminiscing about the excitement of derby day – when the impressive granite structure would be filled with chanting supporters.

Mark has a farm out in Elliot, where he grew up, but since his days with the Sharks he's been based in Durban. That is, when he's not in China marketing his sports-brand company to people half his size. But his roots remain in the Eastern Cape and that is where he intends to return some day. A large part of that decision is to do with his old school. The Andrews have been returning to Selborne for generations. But – heaven forbid for all Selborne scholars – it could easily have been Dale. Grandfather Andrews, deciding that his sons, Kenny and 'Fish', needed to begin their schooling, took it upon himself to embark on a tour of likely institutions. Their first stop was Dale College in King William's Town, but he promptly declared the town to be too hot and continued on his way to coastal East London – where he found the climate more to his liking. And so a tradition began at the illustrious school as Kenny's sons all followed in their father's footsteps. The next generation of Andrews are currently serving their time.

Playing for the first team was one of Mark's greatest achievements. I picked his brain about these early days first, knowing that this fine storyteller was bound to unearth a few gems.

As an athlete Mark first built his reputation in the pool, and was playing Border water polo while still at school. One of his motivations was the tours that the polo team got to go on – where a starving hostel boy could eat to his heart's content in the hotels they stayed in (it was said that he regularly worked his way through the menus twice). It was perhaps this experience – of playing among men from an early age – that allowed him to grow the confidence that would speed his rise to the heights of Springbok rugby, though in his early polo days, this was not a trait always keenly admired. While a fresh first year at Stellenbosch University, Andrews was soon drafted into the Maties first team. He did not quite endear himself to his captain, whose team talks he regularly interrupted with the words: 'In the Border we do it like this ...'

It was also in that year that Mark represented Border at the finals of the Currie Cup B section, during which he inadvertently elbowed a player from the opposing team and was ejected from the water for the remainder of the game. When debating the wisdom of this decision with the referee at the end of the game, the president of the South African Water Polo Association – Mr Doug Sabor – infamously came up to Mark and bellowed: 'Andrews, your glory days are over!'

With his Stellenbosch days behind him, Andrews arrived

in Natal to play rugby there. However, the late Jon Breetzke, who had been busy recruiting for a water polo tournament in Johannesburg, called him in desperation. 'Give rugby a break,' he told Mark, 'you'll never make this year.' A month later Mark was in Argentina making his debut for the Springboks, but before departing he made good on his promise and turned out for Border water polo at the Currie Cup tournament, though he did mention several times that no one should let his dad know he was in Joburg.

I asked Mark to recall some of his early rugby experiences.

'Being selected for your school first team is a huge moment in any South African schoolboy's life,' he told me. 'If you went to a traditional rugby school like I did then getting selected was probably the biggest thing that had happened to you up to that stage in your sporting life. I had played first-team water polo as a 15-year-old and played Junior Springbok water polo by the time I was 16. But all this was nothing compared to how I felt when I was announced as a starting player in Selborne College's first team. What you feel when you are selected to play for the school first team is hard to explain, but it is nothing like when you make the Sharks or Springboks for the first time. Because of the close school community and being present in the school assembly in front of 650 boys and staff when your name is announced, it is a lot more personal than when you open the paper and read that you have been selected to play for the Sharks. There is no fanfare. You sit by yourself and read that you are about to earn your first provincial jersey. But after that assembly it feels like half the school and most of the staff have wished you all the best for your first game. The sense of occasion is so much greater and the euphoria and sense of responsibility awesome. In the professional game of today it is a bit different, in that you get told in front of the team when you get selected for your first game, a bit better than reading of your selection in the paper, but still nothing compared to getting your selection announced in front of the whole school, at assembly.'

Then Mark started to talk about what it was like to play for the Selborne First XV. I could vividly imagine the scene. Eight thousand spectators. The tangible buzz of anticipation around the ground. The boys' growing chant as the stern-looking First XV arrived from their solemn prep at the hostel: 'Jump and jive, come alive, the Selborne team has just arrived. A-ha ha ha ha ...'

'People always thought that how serious and psyched we looked would determine our level of readiness for the upcoming game,' Mark reminisced. 'This was, of course, utter nonsense as I don't think I could have been one iota more serious. My level of focus could not get higher; at times I think I even forgot to breathe while walking because I was so psyched up. As we approached the corner of the field the school cheerleader, who has worn a top hat and coat tails since anyone can recall, would make sure the whole school [remembering that attendance at derby days was compulsory for every boy of the school – no exceptions] was in a level of frenzy that would make a pack of hyenas at a kill look like a tea party.

'We would then sit and for five minutes stare like zombies at the game in front of us, trying to keep our adrenaline in check while waiting for half-time – which would be our cue to go into the change rooms to get ready for the game. There are many things that I learnt about mental preparation when I began playing for the Sharks and the most important thing was that it was okay to be relaxed and talk to people and still be able to put together a coherent sentence. These things were not things I was aware of as a schoolboy and I thought that the more psyched I was the better I would play. I do wish I knew that the more relaxed I was before a game the better I would play, but unfortunately I thought the opposite. This meant that when I took the field I would run the fastest all day for the 30 metres to the halfway line and then the first 10 minutes would be a blur and I could never work out why I always struggled to remember much of the first 10 minutes. I only managed to recall the rest of the game because I had expended all my energy in the first 10 minutes and exhaustion would have begun to set in.

'I recall being so psyched up before one game that at the kick-off I charged off after the ball and, realising I was not going to get there in time, launched myself at the receiver's head. He ducked and I landed metres past him thinking I must have broken something as I couldn't breathe. But being a home game, with the sound of the school going berserk metres away, I pulled myself up while the referee was asking me if I was mad and indicating a penalty to the opponents. Of course, I could not answer as I had severely winded myself but like hell was I going to lie there and look weak so I struggled up, smiled and wobbled back to face the penalty trying to show no weakness.

'I cringe when I think about this now; about how crazy I must have looked. But to the school it just showed how up for it I was – crazy but true!'

Personally, I hold good memories from the rugby games I played on the Selborne fields. Of course, my rare talents – 'rare' in that my rugby talents were rarely ever found – never did grace the main rugby field as Mark's did for three years. Rather, I was included in a scratch 10th team to take on our rivals, Queens and Dale, on some distant swamp known as the Cabbage Patch (located safely on the outskirts of the campus). This wasn't all that bad because as Selborne struggled to raise a 10th team in its open division, a brew of athletics stars, recovering rugby players and hockey lads – most of whom were in matric – were thrown together to take on an *actual* 10th team. Some cricket scores were racked up, not because those taking part had little appreciation or knowledge of the laws of the game, but because most were genuine athletes in their fields.

My appreciation for the oval-balled game, however, began as a blurry-eyed standard six in Norton House, the only hostel of Selborne College. With my twin brother at my side I could take some solace from the fact that I wouldn't face my initiation completely alone. Of course, it was too much to ask of any teenage boy to discern between us (the most unidentical twins to be found) and so, being of a darker hue, I was christened 'Mid Knight' and my flaming red-haired brother was suitably named 'Day Knight'. At Selborne, new hostel boys are collectively known as 'New Pots' and are distinguished by a white button that each has to sew onto his blazer. It is imperative to ensure you have not foolishly chosen too big a button as by the end of the year you have to swallow it as your final New Pot act.[59]

It was at Selborne, from the confines of a boarding house, that I would experience my first real taste of rugby and its place at the centre of every fine rugby school. Touch rugby was played late every afternoon upon the fresh green cricket fields, and it was compulsory for New Pots to join the game. Our task was to cross-cover, and we were threatened with castration should anyone manage to break through the 15 young fullbacks on either side. Early on Saturday mornings, the New Pot chores would include putting the pads on all the uprights, ensuring the corner flags were in place and that the sand buckets were filled up. As the hostel was the rugby heartbeat of the school, all the New Pots would have to be Selborne rugby-song tenors by the end of their first week. And heaven help the young soul who could not name the starting 15 for that Saturday's game.

Ah, the joys of boarding! But those who have survived their boarding sentence will testify that it wasn't all bad and that some of their most memorable experiences and the beginnings of their finest friendships come from this time. When you stick 120-odd boys together, some characters are bound to emerge (especially the mischievous variety). Mark Andrews has learned

82

---

[59] Each New Pot is 'assigned' to a matric in the boarding house, who will be a big brother, looking after him for the duration of the year. In reality this means that the New Pot will ensure 'his' matric does not oversleep before breakfast, that his bed is made and tidied before inspection and that his shoes are polished.

and played many a fine trick; a necessity for any self-professed rugger-bugger.

During the World Cup, evenings off were a rather rare occurrence. So when the team were given some time off, most took full advantage of it. The first such occasion was a reward for beating Australia and Romania in the two opening games. Kitch Christie had broken the Bok squad into two teams, the Green Team and the Gold Team. The Green Team was going to be the team that played the 'midweek' games, like the ones against Romania and Canada, and the Gold Team was the one that was going to play in the so-called 'glory games' – the opening game and any knock-out fixtures, up until the hoped-for final. As both teams had won their first games, Kitch felt a treat was in order.

Now, a night out was a logistical nightmare for the security detail who had the responsibility of maintaining security for all team members throughout the duration of the World Cup. No player was allowed to go anywhere without having an undercover security member with them and with this in mind it was decided to hire out a venue for the team that was in the public domain but that allowed the security detail to coordinate and manage the event. Bertie's Landing, a relatively new restaurant-cum-pub was chosen as the venue, and with much excitement the whole team trooped onto the team bus and off to the V&A Waterfront for a night of festivity.

Those who have been to the V&A Waterfront in Cape Town at any time in the past 15 years would have enjoyed a very different experience to that offered up in 1995. It was in the throes of becoming what it is today – a mixture of a working harbour and shops and bars – and it was not uncommon to be confronted with fishermen offloading their catch a few metres away from you as you walked to a pub or restaurant. However, the smells of freshly cooked seafood must have been heaven for the beefy men who had been restricted to boiled chicken and steamed vegetables for the past two months (though a few of the up-country boys, like Os, stuck to what they knew best and ordered steak instead of what they called 'women's food'). And after not having much, if any, alcohol for almost eight weeks, it did not take long before things were pretty festive. Later, Joel Stransky and Mark, who were roommates, decided to visit an old haunt of Joel's in Sea Point, and after negotiating with one of the security detail, called Doe, off they went.

As dawn approached many Springbok liqueurs later, Doe ordered the return to the hotel. When they arrived, Mark headed off to the team room to find a snack while Joel made his way to bed to catch up on lost sleep. After raiding the team's stash of snacks, fruit and Energade drinks, Mark also made his way to bed on unsteady legs. The sun was just peeking over the horizon when Mark lifted the sheets and collapsed into bed. But as he hit the mattress he realised he was not alone in bed – he could feel slimy skin against his foot and his head was resting against something wet (not to mention the overpowering smell). But it was only when he heard his roommate begin to chuckle that Mark realised he was on the receiving end of a prank. Jumping out of bed and grabbing Joel, Mark proceeded to beat him until he admitted that he had been ambushed as he came to the room by Balie Swart and Rudolph Straeuli, who had overpowered him and 'forced' him to become party to setting Mark up with a new bed mate: a two-metre snoek that had been offloaded from a fishing boat earlier that morning.

As the two miscreants were making their way back to the team coach they had walked past some fishermen who were offloading their catch. They haggled with them for the biggest fish they had, bought it and then headed back to the hotel to look for an empty bed. While walking the passages they had chanced upon Joel, who was on his way to his room. After chasing him down the passage with the bleeding snoek they 'convinced' him that it was in his best interests to allow them to put the fish in Mark's bed.

Having listened to Joel's story, Mark put the snoek out on the balcony, stripped the bed – although the fish blood had by now seeped into his mattress – and climbed back in. Sleep came quickly, despite the lingering smell, and it was not long before everyone was up for the day's activities and the story of the snoek began to spread quickly among the team.

Revenge, however, would be Mark's. That evening, during dinner, he slipped upstairs and got security to open 'my room', telling them that he had 'lost' his key. Leaving the door unlocked, he went and retrieved the now extremely pungent snoek from his balcony and tucked it neatly beneath the sheets and mattress of Balie Swart's bed. Then he snuck back down to dinner.

When Balie returned to his room he smelt a rat, but after much searching he could not discern from where the strange odour was coming. Mark had left the balcony door open – in an attempt to minimise the smell in the room – and Balie surmised that it must be coming from Mark's balcony (two doors down). However, when he finally got into bed, the smell was so overpowering he could not sleep. Eventually, Balie decided to close the balcony door and put the air con on high. After getting back into bed, and with the smell now almost unbearable, he, in desperation, decided to look in his own bed and finally found the rotten fish. Revenge, as they say, was sweet.

Mark may be the Codfather of schoolboy pranks, but the precedent was set by 1938 Lions hard man Blair Mayne. While at a grand Pietermaritzburg ball on the 1938 Lions tour, Mayne was particularly uncomfortable with the formality of the occasion and spent most of his time at the bar. When some Afrikaner farmers invited him to join them on a game hunt, he was only too keen. In fact, he insisted that they set off for the hunt immediately, despite the fact that he was still dressed in tie and tails. He returned at daybreak with an antelope across his shoulders, his suit torn and bloodied from the night's hunt. But he still had enough energy left to plant the bloody carcass in the bed of fellow tourist Jimmy Unwin – who was asleep at the time.

Mark is certainly old school in that sense. No amount of serious rugby – even a World Cup – will stop a rugger-bugger from taking any opportunity to play a prank on one of his mates. However, the story I was really interested in revolved around a 'meeting' days before the World Cup semi-final, and I probed him for details on how the country's finest lock became an eighth man overnight – at a World Cup!

It all began on a Sunday evening, the squad having just reassembled at the Sunnyside Hotel after having been given three days at home (their first leave since they had gotten together two months earlier). It was the final two weeks of the Rugby World Cup, and everyone was excited but tense. Joel and Mark, who had been roommates for the duration of the tournament, were lying on their beds and catching up when the bedroom phone rang. Joel answered. 'Yes, Morné, he is here,' he said after a couple of seconds.

He handed the phone over. 'Markie, can you come to my room please?' Morné asked. He always called Andrews 'Markie'.

Now, this was never a good thing, as all selection meetings took place on Sunday evenings and they almost always took place in Morné's room (as team manager, he usually had the biggest room).

Joel wished Mark luck as although he had played all the main games up to that point, to be called to Morné's room normally meant that you were going to get the news that any player dreads – you were going to be dropped. Mark walked down that old hotel

passage with the same sinking feeling a schoolboy experiences as he makes his way to the headmaster's study for a caning. He stood at the door and took a few moments to compose himself before knocking.

A curt 'Come in!' greeted his rap on the door, and as he entered he saw three gentlemen sitting facing him: to his immediate left was Gysie Pienaar, the backline coach, and on the right was

Morné. Between the two of them was Kitch Christie.

Kitch got right to the point: 'Markie, can you play flank?' he asked.

'No, coach,' Mark replied.

Kitch looked at Mark in a curious way and then asked: 'Are you sure?'

'Yes, coach,' Mark replied immediately. 'I am sure I would remember if I had played flank,' he finished lamely, in a poor attempt at humour.

'That's a pity,' Kitch said, seemingly deep in thought. 'Okay, you can go.'

Mark stood for a second, looked at Morné, who gave nothing away, and then returned to his room with that strange feeling that he had just dodged a bullet (but one which still had his name on it).

Back in their room, Joel swung his legs off his bed and eagerly asked what had happened.

'I'm not sure,' Mark replied.

'You're not sure?'

Mark told him that coach asked if he could play flank and he had told him that he couldn't.

Joel sucked in his breath and shook his head, causing mild panic to sweep through the big lock. 'Well,' he said, 'if he asked you if you could play flank he's obviously not going to play you lock, so saying "no" has probably cost you a place in the semi-final team.'

Mark felt sick and sat on his bed, wondering whether to call his dad and break the bad news, when the room phone rang again. Mark looked at it, knowing already who was on the other end.

This time Mark's walk to the room took even longer – he was, after all, expecting to be informed that his World Cup would not climax quite as planned. However, by the time he found himself outside Morné's room he had accepted his fate. What the hell, he thought. Let me get this over and done with. He knocked once and received the same reception: the curt 'Come in!' Again, the coach fired a question at the big man: 'Markie, can you play eighth man?' he asked.

Mark didn't miss a beat. 'Sure, coach,' he said. 'Eighth man is my best position.'

Kitch whipped around to Morné. 'I told you he could play eighth man,' he said. 'Hell, he is even built like you and you were a great. Markie, you will be a great eighth man!'

'I know, coach,' Mark responded. 'Eighth man is my spot.'

The walk back to his room was a blur; the initial fear of a caning now replaced with apprehension at the thought of an induction as head boy.

'How did it go?' Joel asked as soon as he came through the door.

'I don't know,' Mark replied once again.

'What do you mean? What did they say?'

'Well, coach asked me if I could play eighth man.'

'So what did you say?'

'I said I could.'

'And can you?'

'No.'

Joel peered at Mark. 'Why did you say you could then?' he asked.

'Well, you said they weren't going to play me at lock,' Mark stuttered, 'and I already told them that I can't play flank, so when they asked me if I could play eighth man I said I could.'

Joel stared at him in stunned silence. 'So, are you in the team as eighth man?' he finally asked.

'I don't know.'

On the way back to his room Mark had reasoned that the coaches were trying to figure out how best to plan their bench. If they could put Kobus Wiese on the bench and bring him on early, they could move Mark to eight to keep the line-outs competitive.

Kobus was not renowned as the best jumper around and the French line-out was filled with world-class line-out options.

A restless night ensued.

The next morning, after breakfast in the team room, the coach stood up to announce the team that was going to take the field to play in the World Cup semi-final against the French in Durban.

'Os du Randt, Chris Rossouw, Balie Swart, Hannes Strydom, Kobus Wiese ...'

Mark's heart sank as he realised he had been dropped.

'Francois Pienaar, Ruben Kruger ...'

The names blurred as Mark thought of how he would tell his father he had been dropped for the semi-final.

'Mark Andrews!'

Mark nearly collapsed as he felt the eyes of nearly every player in the room turn on him. He was stunned.

It is tradition that after the team announcement, all the players shake hands with those who have been selected. Andrews received his congratulations, albeit with plenty of disbelief from his teammates, but then he began to panic at the thought of what he had done – putting his own ambitions ahead of the team and country. He approached Christie: 'Coach, I can't play eighth man,' he told him.

Kitch stared at Mark for a second. 'But you said you could play and it was your favourite position,' he finally said.

'Yes, I did, coach,' Mark replied. 'But that was at school.'

The last time Mark had played eighth man was at u14 level.

'Guys,' Christie immediately bellowed across the room, 'we will be leaving for training one hour later than planned.' He then called Francois Pienaar, Rudolph Straeuli (the player who had been dropped for Mark), Morné and Ruben Kruger to the front of the room to teach Mark the basics of playing eighth man. So began the first day of the scariest week of Mark Andrews' rugby life, though at the end of it he would prove himself more than able in one of the greatest days in Springbok rugby history.

Mark Andrews racked up 77 Test caps and was at one time the most capped Springbok lock in history. Many of those caps have been awarded in games against the old foe, the All Blacks. That's a lot of eyeballing, tongue pulling and thigh slapping 'Ka Mates' to face up to.

Mark's first game against the All Blacks was at the 'House of Pain' in Dunedin; a bitterly cold and bleak place to play rugby. For young South African boys with rugby aspirations, the haka is indeed a great rugby occasion, and for Mark it was 'the only dance I ever wanted to attend!' The week's preparations before the first Test were cold and wet; the training hard and physical, with coach Ian Mac warning his men that they would have to 'face up' or 'get stuffed up' – the All Blacks were at that time playing a forward-dominated game which allowed the backs to lie deep and almost slingshot themselves from depth at the Bok defence. The team were psyched up, Mark especially looking forward to a physical encounter and facing his first haka. Incidentally, in the first week of the tour, the team had gone to an original Maori village where the elders explained the significance of the haka. The essence of it is a challenge to battle, effectively saying 'Here we are, this is how we look and this is what we want to do to you. Do you accept the challenge?' It is expected that real men stand and face the haka without emotion and accept the challenge to do battle. To do otherwise shows a lack of respect, and ignoring it, walking away or standing in a huddle is not advisable. So the fact that the old South African anthem was played before that Test, and then the team had to hastily also sing the new anthem, was perhaps not the best start to facing the haka, which was about to begin without them. However, besides getting rucked to near-death at one stage of the game – something that left him with scars he carries to this day – Mark claims that the most painful event of the day was losing the match by a paltry two points.

Mark Andrews was fortunate to play 19 Tests against the All

Blacks and though he never became blasé about the haka, he did learn to enjoy facing it and seeing how the new All Blacks fared in performing it for the first time against the Boks. The All Blacks have a saying that there are two types of All Blacks, those that have played in the All Black jersey and those who have played against the Springboks – the latter being classed as true All Blacks. It is perhaps inevitable then that a wise man of Andrews' lineage would devise a sage response to the fiery jig. Four years on and in a Test to be played in New Zealand, Mark was facing a new young lock named Norman Maxwell who was about to play in his first Test against the Boks. Taking up their customary positions on the 10-metre line and facing the All Blacks 20 metres away, the team stood in single line. At the start of the haka, Mark had noticed, most players walk into position looking down and appear to take no notice of their opponents until 'summoned' by their haka leader. At this point, all the players look up and muster their meanest death stare. So, as Norm lifted his head and fixed his gaze upon Mark, he blew him a kiss. Not being the prettiest of rugby players, Mark recalls a look of panic in Norm's eyes as he tried to keep in time to the steps of the haka, chant the words and maintain his death stare while his opponent blew kisses at him. Norm only managed to regain his composure by breaking his death stare and looking at the bloke next to him. Finally, haka over, there was Mark pitifully shaking his head.

Mark Andrews has an almost boundless collection of rugby tales, but I had to move on. King William's Town beckoned.

AMADODAS

For the first half of my schooling I was an Amadoda. The rugby of Dale College is the heartbeat of sleepy King William's Town and as the traditional rivalries in the Eastern Cape are among the fiercest in the country, these derbies are always something special. On the Border – and particularly between Queens College, Selborne College and Dale College – it gets brutal.[60] Throughout their primary-school years, the Border boys have been smashing each other twice a year. But it's in their final year – for the First XV encounters – that they need to peak.

A return to your old school is a great nostalgic trip, none more so than on Reunion, when old friends gather and compare growing families and receding hairlines. When it's derby day in King, you know it. Black blazers with vertical red strips, and a straw boater for good measure, pour out of Sutton House, Frank Joubert and the other hostels and spread themselves around the school's extensive fields. It's an event that takes the whole day, with the First XV usually only kicking off in the late afternoon when the heat of the day has subsided.

King William's Town, like most towns in this country, loves to raise its own small-town heroes. In my day it was Steven Hall, Luke Smith, Grant Griffiths and Terrence Nicklebein – the latter the finest schoolboy rugby player I have seen.[61] This kind are playing First XV rugby by 16 years of age, and by the end of their first season they've established an alpha male status

---

[60] We called the black-and-white hooped Selbornians Dead Fish and they called us Dead Cats. There were also a good few unpleasant names, chants and songs set aside for the oldest rival, Queens College.

[61] Terrence Knickelbein (1995) holds the Dale record for most tries in a season (25).

among their rugby-crazed peers. They take to physical games a lot quicker than others and soon become your side's only hope of salvation, at least for the coach: 'Everyone, pass the ball to Johnny! It's a team sport, dammit!'

Such sage advice is even more critical at primary-school level, where there is the 'small' problem of freakish early growth spurts. I can recall playing one visiting u10 side that had a beast of a fellow, with a certain Neanderthal appearance, in their ranks. His drooping bottom lip seemed incapable of reaching the rest of his face, and it was rumored that he shaved three times a week. As we warmed up some of the more timid members of the team began exchanging horror stories of some foolish boys who had tried to tackle the Goliath. Each story grew worse than the one before, and it wasn't long before one boy, by the name of Tobias, suddenly began recalling a 'niggling hamstring injury', although he seemed unable to locate the injury and just began massaging all his limbs, grimacing painfully at regular intervals. He audibly pondered whether he may be a 'doubtful starter'.

It was unanimously agreed by the rest of us that it would require two brave souls to attack each of our enemy's thunder thighs and literally hold on for dear life. However, it remained undecided as to which boys would be tasked with such a suicidal mission. The tactical talk had drifted off to Jack Robertson's birthday party later that day when our obese coach waddled up. Surely he could advise his young troops. He'd always been going on about his Rhodesian days; about how 'boys have become so soft these days' and how 'our pale bums would have been skinned like the pathetic runts we were if the Selous Scouts had coached us'. The coach looked us up and down, and slowly shook his head. Then, exhaling a cloud of cigarette breath, he uttered some prophetic words: 'Boys. Tackle low. Bigger they are ...' He wheezed and quickly gulped in a deep breath. 'Harder they fall.'

Then he coughed and spluttered violently. He steadied himself, as if to deliver a quote from Churchill or Doc Craven, but it never came. Finally, after examining us one last time, he shook his head and muttered, 'Good luck.' And then he wobbled off.

Well, the game began, and two enthusiastic sides, naive of most of the rugby laws, climbed into each other. Amazingly, Dale was soon in the ascendency as it turned out that unless the ball was planted in the giant's mitts, he dropped it. And when he did finally set off, clutching the ball, he was thunderously brought to the cloddy ground by a red-and-black swarm. Sebastian Moore even swore that he cried after each tackle.

The game ended in a fine win for Dale. Our coach arrived and gathered us all together. Beaming between deep drags on his cigarette, he said: 'Boys, I would gladly have fought by your sides in the Bush War.'

There was an awkward silence – the hamster on the wheel in our heads was working overtime. None were really certain if this was our first compliment, or if it was sarcasm. Finally, Tobias saluted.

Though my coach was hardly a shrewd tactician, primary-school games can be a great stage for a wily coach. This was proven in another u10 game, this time against Hudson Park of East London. They were given a penalty, and we retreated the usual 10 yards. As they tapped the ball to restart play, they all began blurting out at the top of their lungs, 'Sir, they're not 10 yards!', and advanced swiftly toward us in unison. Being ignorant and perplexed 10-year-olds, we retreated, expecting the discipline of the referee's whistle. The ball-carrier, in the meantime, had hidden the ball inside his jersey, and was hastily making his way up the field towards our try line. We were only saved by a patriotic parent (probably mine), who shouted, 'Wake up, boys! Tackle him!' Someone did and we quickly descended upon the villain like vultures upon a carcass. It was my first experience of the sneaky tactics that are imperative to every good rugby side.

Perhaps the sneakiest Dalian to grace their fields was one H O de Villiers. This was because he rarely kicked the ball, as was the expectation on all fullbacks in the 60s. I had arranged to meet with arguably the greatest Bok No. 15 of all time to gauge his thoughts on his old school and his rugby career.

H O debuted in 1967 against the high-flying France. It was a critical time for the Springboks, and according to Doc Craven the most important Test in Bok history. De Villiers played some of the finest rugby of his life, destroying the myth held by many at the time that, on attack, the fullback was to be seen but not heard – there were few attacking fullbacks in those days (before the likes of H O and J P R Williams). And he only enhanced his reputation on the '69 tour of the British Isles, playing an instinctive, almost reckless roaming role at the back.

My amateurish perception of fullbacks has generally been that of a poor, tortured post-modern soul hanging around near his own goal posts. As he spends most of his time in no-man's-land I'm not even sure that most fullbacks know their own role. Many delight in scoffing at their 'last line of defence' tag when one of them misses the critical tackle that costs their team the game in the final minute. Still, others infuriate us by making graceful leaps to receive a high ball, only to spill it forward with not an opponent in sight. But then along comes a player like H O, or André Joubert, an evolved No. 15 with effortless class.

It was fullbacks like H O that really showcased the attacking potential of the fullback, especially on the '69 tour of the British Isles. However, it was also a tour on which the players felt the brunt of anti-apartheid demonstrations – broken glass and long tacks were often scattered over fields and in Ireland some players were even pelted with potatoes. It was a long and difficult tour, and unfortunately it was also a tour that would prematurely end H O's rugby career. By 27 years of age he'd had 17 operations on his right leg and seven on his left. But by then he had already written his name into rugby folklore.

Today his ebony hair has faded to a greyer hue, but he is still passionate about the game that made him a household name. In terms of his own position in the side, he holds only admiration for the longevity and ability of Percy Montgomery. 'I'm biased when it comes to Percy,' he told me. 'I coached him at SACS. He's a brilliant player.'

And ask him who should replace the man who has been one of the Springbok's greatest servants, and he's convinced it is Francois Steyn. 'He must be groomed for 2011. He is a natural in the position. But the first big hurdle is the Lions tour. It's going to be an exciting tour! We have the talent to beat them but it'll be close.'

It was in the early 1960s when H O learnt his rugby upon the C B Jennings field in front of the harshest of rugby critics.[62] One of them was L L F Wood, otherwise known as 'Charcoal'. Sporting a black Dale cap embroidered with a red heron, the old man, who had arrived as an eight-year-old boarder in 1922, would never miss a single Dale game. And come Monday morning, the First XV coach would be sure to receive a letter wishing his family well, but offering detailed explanation of how Dale needed to improve for the following week's game.

It wasn't only the old Dalians who were keen to offer advice. Neal Hatley, a record-setter in England's Premiership, once fondly recalled how seriously the whole town took home matches. After his first two games in the First XV he was walking into town when a labourer working in one of the gardens stopped him and advised him that the forwards needed to be tighter on the drive, though he did think they showed a lot of promise as a team and could win all of their games that season. As it turned out, Dale only lost once, and very narrowly. That was in a year

---

[62] Old boy C B Jennings played for the Border provincial senior Currie Cup team in 1934 (which shared the cup with Western Province) while still at school. Granted, it was in his sixth season of First XV rugby, but then the burley prop did start playing for the side at only 14 years of age. He became a Bok against the All Blacks in 1937.

when Kenny Ball, the current SACS headmaster, transformed an otherwise average lot into a fine XV. He plucked out the fresh-faced Hatley, a standard nine boy who played eighth man for the fifth team, and stuck him at prop for the first-team. He then picked the eighth-team centre at first-team lock, and the seventh-team eighth man as his lock partner. He left previously first-team players out and filled his side with a number of talented, young players who seemed hopelessly out of position. A lot of the old boys and former first teamers frowned on his selection and doomed the new team to failure, but after a near-flawless season and with nine players in the Craven Week team – including Hatley – they had to eat their own words.

From First XV feats, Hatley moved to Durban, where he formed a friendship with Dickie Muir, an ex-Queens College player. On the afternoon of his first game for Natal – and more than a little intimidated by playing alongside the likes of André Joubert, Wahl Bartmann and Gary Teichmann – he crept into the change room and looked anxiously around for a place to change. Fortunately, Muir saw him and came straight over to make him feel at ease. He kindly showed Neal where he could change before disappearing. But unbeknown to the debutant, Dick had put him in the spot where Rudi Visagie usually changed. The giant man, who hovered near seven foot and easily weighed 140 kilogrammes, promptly put Neal's kit straight in the bin without bothering to find out whose it was. Neal turned to see Dickie laughing away, pulled his kit out of the bin and changed in the shower.

Dale College has come a long way from its humble rugby beginnings in the 1880s, when a hotchpotch of boys and old boys began playing the local Ever Ready Club. And this despite the fact that the school's third headmaster, the Reverend Sutton, took a rather puritanical approach and forbade the game of rugby. He had a terrible habit of appearing unexpectedly on the scenes of any kind of rugger activity, and it only required the words 'Cavy Bob' to be uttered once to magically disperse any forbidden gathering. This, amazingly, after the school had already produced three Springboks and a defiant rebel team (The Shamrocks). This meant that the art of playing rugby had to be learnt elsewhere, mainly by watching senior games played on the nearby Victoria Grounds ('The Grounds' as they were then called). However, when rugby was reinstated a proud tradition grew quickly at the small school.

The Border also boasts a heritage of fine black rugby talent and history.[63] 'The region has enormous playing numbers, but we all know that it's perhaps the worst managed,' H O said. 'There is, I think, a good opportunity to align an academy to Dale College. You've got excellent hostels and facilities already in place, plenty of local talent and a great rugby tradition.'

My time there seems long ago now: those crisp Saturday afternoons broken by the thundering, foot-stomping war cry: 'Aha! Aha! Aha! Kangela e Dale College ...'

Dusk had fallen upon the C B Jennings field and the little frontier town had begun its recovery from a long, hot day. It was time for me to leave.

The N2 stretch that runs parallel to the Wild Coast from Butterworth to Kokstad is particularly exciting – the gauntlet of roaming livestock, potholes and mad truck drivers climaxing in Mthatha. However, I had decided that this time my Golf wasn't up to the challenge, and as I was also keen to make my way north, I took the N6 and pushed on to Queenstown.

---

[63] Journeyman Gcobani Bobo was the first black South African to play for the Dale First XV and the first to win the coveted White Colours Blazer.

OF KUDUS AND SKUNKS

Queenstown is Queens College country. 2008 was the school's 150-year anniversary, and as I drove into town its black and tangerine colours seemed to have been plastered across every vacant wall and hung from every lamp post on the high street. Although it enjoyed an inauspicious start, once Queens College did get going it never looked back, and as if to emphasise its permanence, large white stones spelling out the words *Q College 150* had been arranged high up on the Katberg Mountains overlooking the town – probably the fine work of some unfortunate standard-six boarders.[64]

Because of their fairly isolated locations, schools like Dale College and Queens were largely boarding establishments (many of the pupils being the sons of farmers). And in the early 1900s, these schools could boast of some of the largest boarding facilities in the country. This environment provided any new boy, or 'Skunk', with a series of tough initiations.[65] For a start a new boy, ignorant of the school's traditions, would soon be awoken from their slumbersome summer holiday when through the post would come a Queens history book which, he would be informed,

---

[64] C E Ham, who was the school's first headmaster, left rather promptly for financial reasons (boys returning from their July holidays in 1864 found no teacher present and the school building closed and awaiting a new tenant).

[65] For years the new boys were known as 'Skunks', but recently this term has been bravely banished and with it any related 'malpractice'. The purpose of Skunking – often forgotten – is that a new arrival has a senior who will look after him. The primary duties were amazingly motherly: a Skunk would have to wake up five minutes earlier than his Skunk Masters to wake them up gently and have their clothes ready. If they were feeling especially tired, the Skunk would go down to the House kitchen and make them breakfast and then make their beds, pack their books for school and refer them to their timetable to see which class they had first.

must be keenly studied for the all-important New Boys' Test (pass mark, 70 per cent). Forget finding the coolest Space Case before you crack on at senior school; this Test was the only thing that mattered at that point – something that would indicate to the rarely pleased seniors that you knew something about the school and its traditions.

However, this was just the beginning. The real initiation took place within the confines of the boarding house. Ian Dorrington once recalled his Skunk experience in the mid-60s:

> Part of this process consisted of a specific occasion when together with the other new boys, but individually, you had to run the length of the dormitory, with all the older Skunks armed with cricket bats, tackies or slip-slops, or any other suitable item to hand, which would then be used to hit you. This was until you reached the end of the room, where some of the bigger boys would anyway hold you up and really whack you. I can tell you, one would run and dive to reach the end of that room. Once there, you had to tell a joke, which was usually pretty weak and the guys would jeer and boo. Then you had to sing a song and run back through the gauntlet again before you could get out of the dorm.[66]

Reminiscing about these kinds of experiences as an old boy is one of the great pleasures of having been at a traditional boarding school, no matter the pain or panic at the time.

An early initiation into the traditions of the school for all Skunks would take place during the first sing-song practices of the new term, where the school would holler out rugby songs and war cries until the head boy and cheerleaders were appeased. Those with as yet unbroken voices would respond enthusiastically and fearfully to the cries of the cheerleader. Between cursing the legions in East London and King William's Town the war cry

---

[66] Ian Dorrington (1965 matric). Neil Veitch, *Queen's College 1858-2008: In This, Her Honour*, p. 153.

and favourite songs like 'Rum and Coca-Cola', 'Glory, Glory' and 'Sausages' would reverberate through the school:

What are we going to do with them, Queens?
Skin them and eat them alive!
Skin them and eat them alive!
What? Sausages?
No! Dalians!

Of course, it wasn't long ago that corporal punishment at almost all South African boys' schools was the norm for even minor offences like shirt sleeves which weren't rolled up three fingers above the elbow or socks that had fallen down. One respected Queens deputy headmaster, now the fine rector of Grey High, was Neil Crawford. Revered by the boys and respected by the parents, he grew a reputation of incredible commitment to the school. But it was his reputation as a disciplinarian that earned him his nickname: 'Battie'. Rumour had it that after allowing the miscreant to choose the cane – all of different widths and lengths – that would shortly greet his nervous backside, Crawford would stride forward towards his prone victim like a batsman advancing down the wicket, his gown wafting up behind him like a cape. It was said that if you looked back as he approached he looked rather like Batman. Hence the nickname.

There is no doubting that such stories almost always exaggerate the truth, but there is also no doubting that the masters and teachers with the most fearsome disciplinary reputations are often those revered and most liked by the boys. As too many new teachers learn, an undisciplined classroom is often indicative of a teacher lacking respect from his or her class.

By the end of your standard seven or grade nine year – your initiations far behind you – your fagging duties would end, and though the world of the boarding house may have defined a young lad looking to assert and discover himself, so too had the great game of rugby.

I played my first kaalvoet rugby game on their fields, at outside centre. My father spent the evening before explaining to me exactly where such a position needs to stand, though at that age positions tend to be rather meaningless when all 30 boys flock to the ball. It was just a game then, far from the seriousness of later school years when results had bearing upon the Monday mood. For Queens, one could say the First XV results even affected the town, for 'What is good for Queens, is good for Queenstown!'

There are good reasons for a Queens boy to strive for First XV accolades, not least of which is the opportunity to increase your chances with the girls of GHS. But the other is that while most Queens teams play in a black-and-orange striped jersey, the First XV don an all-white jersey.[67] The 1984 side, with the talented Daryll Cullinan, was arguably the finest ever Queens College side. However, Cullinan's talent had been clear for all to see a year earlier at the Border Schools' Rugby Day in 1983. Queens had the policy that on such a day individualism would not be tolerated; the first priority was for the team to win and under no circumstances was an individual to shine at the expense of the team. During the scrappy match, Queens were awarded a penalty just behind the halfway line. Daryll approached his captain and said that he could 'slot' the penalty from there, roughly 20 yards in from the touch line. Cullinan was an extremely gifted kicker of the ball, and with the game near its end, the captain declined the option, perhaps partly because of the philosophy of no one individual sticking out. A short, heated discussion followed, but the captain insisted that Queens should run the ball. Daryll eventually conceded and got in line. The scrum half proceeded to

---

[67] Note that if you're the outside centre, you'll be wearing the number 16. Queens have played without a No. 13 jersey since the tragic death in 1951 of Victor Maitland, who wore the No. 13 jersey for the First XV that year. He was travelling back from Cape Town after watching a Test match there. Of interest, however, is the fact that Maitland was a prop and not a centre. In those days, the fullback wore the number 1 and the wings were 2 and 3. Thus, the props wore 13 and 15.

tap the ball and pass it down the line to the fly half – Cullinan. Daryll took the ball just inside of the Queens 10-yard line and let fly with the most superb drop kick, which sailed through the middle of the posts for three points!

The net result of that was that Daryll did not play rugby again for that year, a decision that cost Queens a good fly half, but one that also allowed Daryll to concentrate on his cricket, and the rest, as the cliché goes, is history.

Today, like Dale College, the majority of scholars at Queens are black. The rivalry between the two, however, remains healthy as new arrivals inherit age-old traditions, and the Dale College game always seems to have just a little extra spice, especially on Reunion Weekend.

From the school magazine, *The Queens Quire*, to its active old-boy unions, Queens College marches on – black and orange colours, kudus and song books uniting old boys of all ages, colours and creeds. Cecil John Rhodes had it spot on when he said: 'All these Queenstown boys are good. They all turn out well.'

Between the Border triangle of Dale, Queens and Selborne, and the Grahamstown triangle of Kingswood, St Andrew's and Graeme College, you have a history of rugby rivalry that has bred numerous Springboks over the years. The old Cape Colony may have been the first to pick up the pig's bladder in South Africa, but the game grew rapidly and spread quickly to the farms and cities of the interior and beyond. And if there is one school in South Africa where the game was seen as manna from heaven it was Grey College of Bloemfontein. From Queenstown, via ancient Aliwal North, I would make my way to the country's geographical and rugby grassroots epicentre.

IV

THE SPRINGBOK
NURSERY

Grey College

August 2008

RUGBY RECIPE

Bloemfontein. A place so flat you can see your dog running away for 3 days. The closer my Golf wheezed to the city, the less significant habitation there seemed to be. The tarmac ribbon winds past flat, dusty veld, its endlessness punctuated only by the occasional water windmill. Then, suddenly, the oasis of Bloemfontein appears; a city steeped in history and rugby. There may even be more rugby fields in Bloem than there are Dutch Reformed Churches, such is the passion of the rugby zealots in this central chunk of the country. In fact, true blasphemy here is a local who confesses ignorance of the great game. They are proud of their heritage and culture, especially when grassroots rugby is mentioned. Grey College is South Africa's undisputed rugby nursery. The old school has set the standards in schoolboy rugby for nearly seven decades, and continues to raise the bar.

Grey College sounds far too English for Bloemfontein and, in fact, it is named after a remarkably popular Englishman, if that is not an oxymoron in some quarters. The popular Englishman in question was Sir George Grey – soldier, explorer, writer and politician. Governor of New South Wales, governor of New Zealand and prime minister of New Zealand, he was also, importantly, governor of the Cape Colony from 1854 to 1861. Born in Lisbon in 1812 a few days after his father had been killed fighting Napoleon's forces at the Siege of Badajoz (a siege at which, incidentally, William Webb Ellis's father was also killed), Grey became the most popular governor of the Cape of all time, loved by Brit, Boer and tribesman alike. His sphere of activity took him far beyond the Cape to Natal, Basutoland (as Lesotho then was called) and the Orange Free State. He instituted great public works, including libraries, hospitals and schools, and in 1855 he gave the money to start Grey College – 5,000 pounds. It was his own money! At the same time he got the Grey Institute in Port Elizabeth going, Grey High School as it became.[68]

As I hit the outskirts of the city I began to remember the train trips we used to take up to Bloemfontein: packed in like cattle on the Friday afternoon, disembarking early the next morning with little or no sleep and being herded off to a host for a breakfast of boerewors, eggs and rare steak – and all before 7am! Before the game we were always treated like royalty and made to feel completely at home, but during the contest that followed we were battered into submission (and usually on the receiving end of between 50 and 120 points). A single try against Grey College has always been tantamount to a near victory. So, as Grey would be satisfied with their 75-3 drubbing of us (my ninth-team experience), so too were we more than content with our paltry three points, considering it sufficient evidence to declare 'a draw' (though not within earshot of a navy Grey blazer).

With little sleep on the way up to Bloemfontein and having been on the receiving end of a thumping from the hosts, the return

[68] Grey also founded the school traditionally considered the finest rugby school in New Zealand – Auckland Grammar. They share the same motto as Grey – *Stabilis* (meaning steadfast) – and a school badge. Historically, Auckland Grammar has had more All Black representatives than any other school in New Zealand. They also hold the record for the most old boys in one team at a World Cup: four at the RWC in 1987. The four were the Whetton brothers, Grant Fox and John Kirwan. It should be noted, however, that Gisborne Boys' High have, in recent years, consistently been New Zealand's finest rugby school.

home was as exciting as a trip in a hearse. Many a philosophical rugby player pondered on that solemn Sunday mourning return why they had come up short *again*. A few theories were always offered up – some put Grey's success down to its old corrugated-iron-roofed tuck shop that enforced a diet of red meat at each break time, while others claimed that initiation for a standard six boarder involved sleeping with his gum guard and shoulder pads until he has been transformed into a hulking rugby beast a year or two later. But none of them were ever convincing.

Of course, if your First XV does ever happen to win in Bloemfontein then this will transform your return trip. Suddenly, sleep-deprived boys will be thundering out war cries, echoing the school song in unison from their carriage windows as they depart the station, and will still be rasping hoarsely as they arrive home. Sunday truly will be the Day of Rest.

Such victories, however, are considered Acts of God. But then a loss is not always bad for any youngster. You'll certainly grow more through defeat than victory (which, incidentally, was the message I was trying to drum into our Grey opponents when I was stuck at the bottom of a vigorous maul).

It would be almost impossible to explain why rugby is so competitive in South African schools – and in Grey's in particular – without dipping into the roots of the game, and that means relocating to the cobbled streets of Edinburgh about 140 years ago. After all, it was the Scottish schools, far more so than their English counterparts, who most epitomised muscular Christianity:

Almond, for 40 years headmaster of Loretto, proclaimed the aim of producing "a race of robust men, with active habits, brisk circulation, manly sympathies and exuberant spirit". Merchiston, famed for its combined forward play in spite of having only 130 pupils, developed these attributes through constant compulsory practice, Spartanism – rising at seven for a walk or run followed by a cold bath – and elementary sports science. Each boy was weighed and measured twice a term. Almond believed that the Scottish schools had the advantages of pupils with hardier upbringings and an enthusiasm generated by regular matches against others, while the battle to win team places that gave boys "a certain degree of school position" created an understanding of the self-denial and commitment needed.[69]

Training for a place in the Grey College First XV begins during the first week of the fourth term – the cricket term (after the rugby season has barely ended!). Two open groups of 90 players follow an intensive conditioning and skills-training program before trials are finally held in February. Come rugby season, Grey have 28 teams across four age groups, and its First XV have finished undefeated in nearly half of their rugby seasons in the last four decades. The 2007 team, with the Ebersohn twins at the forefront, averaged 55 points a game, the highest in the school's history. That was also the year the Springboks, for the first time in rugby history, fielded a front row from the same alma mater – three old Greys. Later that year, five were in the match 22 for the World Cup final. It is not surprising then that Grey College is known as the Springbok nursery. The great rugby schools of Paul Roos and Bishops may have more Boks on their honours boards (though most were pre-World War II), but Grey has, for decades, done a fine job of consistently nurturing the next crop of the country's finest, for which the Sharks have long been grateful.

Success would seem to breed success, and this is most evident in Reunie Hall rather than upon their rugby fields. Erected with funds provided by old Greys, Reunie is *the* very heart of the school; where the Grey apprenticeship begins. Here boys assemble on Mondays and Fridays and are regularly addressed by well-known personalities. On the walls are honours boards

---

[69] Huw Richards, *A Game for Hooligans: the History of Rugby Union*, p. 47.

bearing the names of those who gained first-class matric passes and merit awards as well as the names of school captains and sport captains. Various trophies won by the school together with the national colours of the many old Greys who have represented their country are displayed in cabinets that line the walls. The hall breathes achievement, and is perhaps a place where the meek could quite easily grow an inferiority complex, but it is in this space that the spirit and tradition of Grey becomes tangible. So much so that it was chosen as the venue for Hansie Cronje's funeral.[70]

Hansie, himself an old Grey, had sent a fax to the headmaster, Johan Voldsteedt, only two days before his tragic death in late May 2002, after watching an awesome game between Affies and Grey in Pretoria (which, incidentally, included a number of boys who would later play beside each other at the 2007 World Cup). The fax mentioned, among other things:

> To find attractive rugby on the TV is impossible, but 60 minutes of watching you on Saturday was enough to last me another winter ... how I wish that 15 years would not go so fast.[71]

Success is always collective. It requires the advice, wise or otherwise, of a coach to mould and shape you. If ever there

---

[70] His father, Ewie Cronje, was the Grey rugby cheerleader of the late 1950s. The qualification for being a school's rugby cheerleader is rather straight forward: he must be one unlikely to ever compete for a place in the First XV and he must be an extroverted character dedicated not only to making a fool of himself but also of the opposition. In short, he is the heartbeat of the school at sing-song and during the First XV game.

[71] Cronje himself played Craven Week rugby. It seems to be common that the talented boys around the country are gifted in both major sporting codes. Seven Springboks have also played cricket for South Africa – H. H. Castens (captain at rugby and cricket), Biddy Anderson (cricket captain), Percy Jones, Jimmy Sinclair (who also played soccer for South Africa), Alf Richards (captain at rugby and cricket), Jackie Powell and Tony Harris – and 24 have played provincial cricket, the most recent being Morné du Plessis and Helgard Muller, both old Greys.

was a no-nonsense coach, it was 'Lappies' Labuschagne. Poor form or a lack of dedication upon the pitch and the coach would threaten his players with being dropped. And he meant it. He once banished a player from the high-and-mighty First XV to the bowels of the seventh team.

In 1988, a fine Grey side was due to play Paarl Gimnasium in the final of the Volkskas Shield. While in a huddle in their change rooms, and only minutes from kick-off, the Paarl Gim boys erupted for some reason next door. Unamused, Ruben Kruger shouted a few swear words in their direction at the same moment as Lappies entered the changing room. A deadly hush descended as Lappies stared coldly at each player in turn. Then he turned and walked out.

Lappies rarely had to say much to make a point, and perhaps the quietly spoken Ruben Kruger learnt more discipline from this coach than he ever did against a Paarl Gim or All Blacks pack.

There can be nothing worse than performing poorly against the local school *on the other side of the train tracks.* In 1986 an average local side was beaten by Grey in an awful display of rugby. After the game Lappies entered the changing rooms and declared: 'If this is the type of rugby that you want to play you can coach yourself. I am done.' And he left, true to his word. No coach appeared for practice that week. But the following Saturday, after a much-improved game, he entered the change rooms and declared his retirement from retirement: 'You're not so bad after all,' Lappies told the boys. 'I will coach you again'.

Coach Lappies would make his intentions and requirements absolutely clear from the onset of the season. Each Grey boy knew exactly what was expected. So much so, that the coach spent many afternoons in his car, paging through the local paper, *Die Volksblad*, whilst the boys sweated and trained before him – each boy carried enough fear and respect for the man to know that their training could not drop a single notch in intensity.

Coaches are the first ingredient for a school's successful rugby recipe. They are rugby people with heart and soul for the game. The humble Dries van der Wal followed Lappies. He always wore a little blue hat and carried a booklet in which he would write down the score (and tries) as the game unfolded. But despite his quaint eccentricities he was a coach that constantly sought to improve the school's administration of the game, the coaching structures, and enhance his players' natural abilities. The First XV now has a forwards' and a backline coach, both members of the school staff. There are two biokineticists. One is responsible for the players' conditioning and strength and the other specialises in skills coaching and the team's defensive play. Grey has a physiotherapist who evaluates and assesses injuries after each game and refers injured players to an orthopaedist if necessary. There are supervised gym sessions and players are required to eat balanced diets (as well as being given a specific pre-match meal prior to each game, as recommended by a dietician). There are regular weighings and monitoring before and after each game, and any weight loss will be counteracted by proper supplements. Rugby has certainly changed with the times:

THEN	NOW
Coach carts the boys off in a banged-up, rusting school bus/ cattle truck that all pray will make it there, let alone on time.	Posh, luxury buses hired. First XV usually travel in their own bus and some have been known to fly to games.
30 minutes before game: Begin warm-up with strawberry Steri Stumpie to raise energy levels. Possibly a boerie role as well, to see you through.	*Two hours before game:* Down third energy supplement drink of the morning. Meet with team in quiet room to discuss tactics.

10 minutes before game: Gather team and take light jog to the nearest poles and back, followed by some stretches (any will do so long as it looks like something is being strained).

Final team talk: This is usually about girls. Some war cry to show your opponents you're more than ready.

Game on: Usually both sides come out firing, but the action soon settles into *a comfortable rhythm* that both sides are far more accustomed to.

After game: Find dad = money for tuck shop.

40 minutes before game: Intense warm-up begins. Plenty of stretching of muscles that few knew existed, whilst putting on a cold, focused stare.

Final team talk: This involves phrases like 'Do it for College!' Some are brought to tears.

Game on: Intense and violent. Each time there is a break, physios, masseurs and a swarm of boys with water bottles descend upon the players.

After game: Warm-down exercises. Find agent = money for tuck shop.

Of course, the 'Then' column still remains the rule for all those sane fellows that languish in the bottom teams of their age groups. But for the serious, rugby has become saturated with money. Every starting First XV player, and a good few below, stands a strong chance to grow a mad game into an even madder career.

THE WORLD CUP WINNERS

Genealogy has always played its role in South African rugby. That the game is passionately embraced is beyond doubt, and so it is not surprising to see family names crop up time and again, generation after generation.

There are families with many Springboks caps. South Africa has had three sets of three brothers – the Luyts, the Bekkers and the Du Plessis. The three Luyts – Richard, Freddie and John – uniquely played together in the same Test. They did it twice – against Scotland and Wales in 1913. There have been 30 sets of Springbok brothers, the most recent being Jannie and Bismarck du Plessis who have World Cup medals to prove it.[72]

Raised in Bethlehem, the Du Plessis brothers had family that had been to Grey. Bismarck's rise at Grey was especially rapid – and, in fact, he never lost a game in a Grey rugby jersey.

The hooker is that poor soul stuck in the middle of the scrum who is meant to 'hook' the ball back when it is put in at the scrum. But Bismarck is perhaps most appreciated when he launches another demented run through, or over, his opponents. He is in every way the caricature of the snorting tearaway hooker and I am sure that his Grey teammates took particular pleasure in pointing him in the direction of the quivering opposition. In fact, by the time he became a Bok, he was soon deemed too good to gather splinters and usurped the hooking position from his own captain. That's because he may just be the best in this new

---

[72] In addition, nine father-and-son pairings have played for South Africa. Ruan Pienaar became the most recent son (Schalk Burger being the one before him). Felix and Morné du Plessis are unique in South African rugby history in that both father and son captained the Boks. They were unique in the world till Anton Oliver captained the All Blacks.

hooking business. Parts of the game have certainly changed. Were Bismarck born 10, 50 or 100 years ago, he may have enjoyed legal hacking, or been penalised for 'foot up', but of course, always denying culpability as is the prerequisite for such a position.[73]

Bismarck is certainly no nickname, though it did get my mind going. Here are some of those more memorable nicknames that have graced rugby programmes and paper columns over the years:

Fairy	-	Barry Heatlie
Uncle Fester	-	Keith Wood
Bummer	-	Bob Scott
Darkie	-	D. R. Bedell-Sivright
Noddy	-	Fran Cotton
Shaggy	-	Will Greenwood
Axel	-	Anthony Foley
Billy Whizz	-	Jason Robinson
Buzz Lightyear	-	Jeremy Davidson
The King	-	Barry John
Iron Man	-	Jack Matthews
Judith	-	Craig Chalmers

Some memorable Springbok nicknames include: *Mary* Jackson, *Piston* van Wyk, *Cowboy* Saunders, *Carrots* Geraghty, *Okey* Geffin, *Chum* Ochse, *Jakkals* Keevy, *Klippies* Kritzinger, *Bullet* Dalton, *Lem* Honiball, *Mof* Myburgh, *Slaptjips* Rossouw, *Domkrag* Erasmus, *Cocky* Hahn, *Vleis* Visagie, *Bingo* Burger, *Salty* du Rand and *Stompie* van der Merwe. My own lineage also boasts one *Saturday* Knight, who played for the Springboks in 1912-13.

---

[73] 'Hacking' is defined as tackling a player carrying the ball by kicking him. It was banned in the 1870s to make the game safer, though rugby remained a rather dangerous sport. There were 71 deaths of rugby players in Yorkshire alone in three seasons in the early 1890s.

On either side of the hooker are the porky props, and Jannie du Plessis has enjoyed the aroma of his older brother's armpits for a good few years now – first with the Sharks and now with the Springboks. But their first and only game together at Grey College arrived in Jannie's final year. As rugby fate would have it, Jannie's last year had an enormous effect on his rugby future. In his final year at Grey, and after an overseas tour to Argentina, Dries van der Wal dropped him from the 'Cherries' to the Third XV.[74] Jannie was livid, knowing he had a greater desire to play for the Cherries than his replacement, and he let the great coach know it, poking him in the chest while making his point. But after domino injuries in the First and Second XV, Jannie was promoted to the Free State Craven Week side, and after returning to the school, he again received the First XV jersey.

Grey College is perhaps the most competitive environment in which to make a school's first team anywhere in the world. Achievement also bestows privilege at the school: The first team has its own dressing room, which no other team is allowed to use. The first-team is also the only team who is allowed to train on the main rugby field with practice jerseys – all other sides wear their Grey jerseys (and if you're a boarder, there's a good chance it is still soaked in sweat from the last four games). Finally, only the first-team players are allowed to wear white laces in their boots. All the other teams have to wear different coloured laces – a tradition that dates back many years.

I'm sure the Cherries aren't too stroppy as they watch Grey's finest practice in their fancy colourful jerseys and polished, white-laced boots. The Second XV have, after all, inherited a traditional name that hails from a legendary train journey in September 1946 – suffice it to say that there was an ample supply of cherry liqueur on that particular trip. And they've also got their own boot laces. Orange has been in vogue since 1965,

---

[74] The Grey Second XV are traditionally called the 'Cherries' for reasons that will be explained later in this chapter.

prior to a game in Queenstown.[75] Apparently, 'there were quite a few "wows"' when the boys took to the field with their new bootlaces for the first time.[76]

Rugger-buggers may be a refined breed but the front-row fatties are an altogether unique species. They seem to treasure each scrum down as if it were a special occasion. You could swear they actually enjoy it. A traditional prop would tell you that this is the only part of the game that matters, and that even if his team were roundly thrashed, he couldn't care less because he popped his opposite number three times. And how the perception of the role of the front rower has changed. In days gone by, it would have been quite acceptable for a prop to admit to never having gone beyond a brisk walk in his rugby career. He would have been forgiven for reasoning that there are benefits to standing in one place on the field, as the game will eventually come his way. But there is a new breed of 'mobile prop' that no longer drops the ball at a maul, but drops it on the wing instead. In fact, this breed has forgotten the very core of their job on the field. From the days when a prop could be successful without even touching the ball, he has now convinced himself that he is able to run like a winger and kick grubbers like a string-pulling No. 10. The result is that he can no longer scrum. Thankfully, Grey College is still producing burly forwards with an ability to heave in the scrum and pass both to the left and right.

---

[75] Before Grey travelled to all corners of South Africa they enjoyed a fierce rivalry with Queens College – whose First XV enjoyed a number of notable successes against the Grey Colossus in the 70s and 80s. But for Grey to maintain its standards these days, it needs to travel far and wide to seek out strong opposition. Annually, it competes against Affies, Pretoria Boys' High, Selborne College, Grey High School, Glenwood, Paarl Boys' High and Paul Roos.

[76] Mich Engelbrecht and a fellow pupil, Ezra Cilliers (now a well-known dentist in Bloemfontein), were regular members of the Cherries and wanted to adopt something distinct – like cherries on their jerseys – but 'the authorities would not allow it'. While sitting in Mr Kallie's German class, where many a great thought was dwelt upon, the idea of orange boot laces came to the pair.

Playing in the front row also requires the acting ability of a seasoned professional on the West End. Forget melodramatic prima donnas like Christiano Ronaldo, these heavyweights are some of the finest actors in professional sport. Those bemused looks when a penalty goes against them after an 'accidental collapse' are absolutely priceless. Commentator Bill McLaren was spot on when he said, 'Props are as crafty as a bag of weasels.' To their credit, though, they do know a good deal more than the ref about what goes on in those mysterious dark recesses of the scrum. If anything, the first criteria for a Grade 1 Referee Qualification should be some form of front-row experience.

Another World Cup medal winner and another in a long line of beefy front row forwards from Grey College is C J van der Linde. I remember watching C J, the schoolboy, at a game in Bloemfontein, against the visiting Selborne College. Selborne, on their previous two visits to Bloem, had won both First XV games. However, with C J in the Grey side a third victory seemed an impossibility. 'He's at least 140 kilogrammes, runs the 100 metres in 10 flat, and bench presses a cow with either arm,' some starry-eyed standard six whispered to me the morning before the match, looking cautiously over each shoulder. And before you knew it, the rumour was growing with each passing hour.

Of course, the myth was dealt a somewhat cruel blow. That's because his game was ended rather prematurely by the opposing prop, Michael Coetzee, who landed rather heavily on C J's back. The Grey juggernaut was forced to leave the field on a stretcher after barely a minute's play. Coetzee subsequently left for rugby in France, where he would be certain to avoid retribution from C J.

C J van der Linde seems a stereotypical prop. They are usually distinguished by:

1. *Shaven head and lack of neck;*
2. *As tall as they are wide;*

3. A minimal weight of 120 kilograms and an average height of six foot;

4. An excellent uppercut which is often the cause for their move from the back row to the front row;

5. An ability to loiter on the wing for large portions of the game.

Francois Steyn, like the Du Plessis brothers, was also educated at primary school in Bethlehem. Despite his enormous talent and potential at such a young age, he was too small, so his coach, Oom Marius Grobler, lied about his age to push him into the Eastern Free State primary-schools team for Craven Week. I first saw him playing against Paul Roos in Stellenbosch. Grey won an otherwise morbid game, but I do remember the tall fly half's boots launching the leather ball the length of the field – it was Steyn, nicknamed 'Lootpoot' (Leadfoot) at the time. Little could he have known that he would still be a teenager when he won the World Cup, or go on to play in every backline position barring scrum half in the green jersey.

In contrast, Ruan Pienaar, the last of the five old Greys to get a hand on the World Cup in 2007, began as a scrum half before the Larkham comparisons began and a lack of a successor to Butch James' throne sent him to fly half. Young and extremely gifted, he is perhaps too versatile for his own good and it has been a temptation for coaches to use him – like Steyn – to fill just about every jersey in the backline.

So, five Grey College old boys were World Cup winners in 2007. And more are surely on their way: Brüssow, Stegmann, Ebersohn. But the thing that commends them more than any 'stat' is what their proud rivals have to say about them. I have heard more times than I care to remember how a past victory over Grey College was a defining moment in this or that season. This speaks volumes for the esteem in which Grey College rugby is held.

V

THE LIONS ARE COMING

Club rugby

September 2008 – April 2009

I left Bloemfontein's dry heat for the dark, cold and wet of a British winter. It would have been a fearful pilgrimage were it not for the fact that half of South Africa was already there – the south-west of London is especially colonised, and suburbs like Wimbledon are now commonly referred to as 'Wimblefontein'. I arrived in time for the start of the new academic year. The only South African authors who can enjoy writer's block for a living are those writing self-help books and this meant that my profession would have to remain education for the time being – I'd be teaching English to the English for the next six months.

The school rugby season had ended in South Africa, and the only 'real' rugby that remained were the closing stages of the Currie Cup. Sky Sports would have to suffice. There was also the upcoming Boks year-end tour, which would send me to the great British rugby stadiums (as well as offering some insight into the coming Lions tour), but a British safari would not be complete without venturing into the heart of club rugby.

RUGBY FOR AMATEURS

East Anglia's pancake plains would rival the Free State for any Flat Earth Society Award. Situated an hour or two to the north-east of London, this place was to be my home until Christmas. I had accepted a temporary teaching position in a small village called Thurston, a place just big enough to have its own pub and – bless their dorp souls – a rugby club: *Thurston Rangers* to be exact (or so the spartan clubhouse announced). The rugby club lay on the outskirts of the village. Surrounded by farmland – small, hedged fields – it would have been largely invisible but for the distinctive woodwork that graced either end of the two pitches that ran parallel to the clubhouse. There were no stands and no advertising. It smacked of no-frills amateur rugby. Perfect.

The club's website gave me more than a little to digest. The picture of their club president was one of a middle-aged bloke with a Jackson 5 Afro doing his finest rapper pose. However, they had won their division the previous year, so there must be some degree of serious rugby played at the club. The website also declared that early-season training had already begun and would continue the following Tuesday.

Some light pre-training touch rugby was on the go when I arrived at the club three days later. I joined in immediately, eagerly looking for some brave stranger to pass the ball to me.

'Oi, girls! Let's stop the poofter rugger and get on with some training. Come in!' Spunky, our club coach, bellowed. Short, stocky and shaven headed, 'Coach Spunky' (I never did learn his real name) apparently had an impressive military background and I also suspected that he might be Brian Moore's twin.[77] By

---

[77] Remember him? He was that feisty, pit bull of a hooker, who looked far more like a French forward.

day Spunky was a prison warden but by night he transformed into an even meaner coach.

Twenty or so rugby oafs of all shapes and sizes gathered on the sidelines around Spunky. There was Olly, the club captain and a man-mountain of a second-rower. Next to him was Andy, an (already) exhausted prop forward whose belly had begun to outgrow his worn school jersey, and Phil, a burly, unshaven flanker, who would not have looked out of place on *America's Most Wanted*. And then there was me: a gangly, 'somewhere-in-the-backline' hopeful. I knew that if I was going to win the respect of this hardened lot, I'd have to put on my deepest, manliest voice and offer plenty of advice that began with 'Back in South Africa, we did it like this . . .' and (if I was feeling really confident) ended with 'And that's pretty much what won us the World Cup. Twice.'

Two hours later I was exhausted. I had been under the impression that, by definition, an amateur club implied at least half the practice would be touch rugby or stretching, not constant fitness work and tackle bags.

'So, mate, where do you play? Wing?' Spunky asked me as I dragged my tired limbs from the field.

He probably assumed I was the type of guy who played to keep his kit clean for following week's game, I thought as I watched him quizzically surveying my lanky frame. He would not have been that far off. 'Ja, somewhere out there, I reckon,' I said.

'Good. The Seconds have a home game on Saturday. Be here by midday to warm up.'

Though the club only managed to muster two sides, by Saturday afternoon I was becoming quietly excited at the prospect of putting on a rugby jersey. All my unfulfilled ambitions in the game would now surely be put to rest in my first start since my glory days for the school's 10th XV, I decided. Well, almost my first start. Keith, our 45-year-old fly half and captain, tossed me the No. 17 jersey in the change rooms, and told me to be ready to sub for 9-15. I felt a bit like the boy that's picked last for the playground game at school break, but I consoled myself with the idea that once I got onto the field my (as yet untapped) Habana-esque potential would see me soon classified upon the Thurston Rangers website as 'foreign find of the season'.

A pleasant afternoon in England is one when it doesn't pour with rain. Despite the bitter chill in the air – heralding the beginning of winter – there was some weak sunshine, so the match was deemed to be kicking off in 'fine conditions'. However, despite this, less than half a dozen spectators had braved the cold to see an epic unfold.

For 40 minutes, my contribution didn't extend much beyond carrying water bottles, though as the average age of our pack was 48, I was kept fairly busy. We were up against the younger Lowestoft and Yarmouth Rugby Football Club, from the north-east coast of Suffolk, though Keith and his 46-year-old halfback partner, Tony, were playing a blinder. Phil, the mad flanker, was also doing a fine job of stealing the ball, mostly from the opposition, and copping a few boots and fists for his efforts, while Duncan, our burly No. 8, kept up a piercing monologue (whether he be at the bottom of a ruck or taking a breather on the wing) – 'C'mon, Thurston! Dig deep, boys! They're wilting now, boys!' et cetera – irrespective of whether they were wilting or not.

At half-time, Duncan barked out a charged team talk beneath our poles, though his exhortation (mostly expletives) was so loud that it seemed to be for most of Suffolk. It's largely a blur to me, however. All I wanted was to get my hands on the ball and run with it; to join a manly game of rugger.

And then, the call-up: 'Matt. Come on at right wing.'

I'm no racehorse and have no finishing qualities to speak of, but I saw enough of the ball to make me happy. Once again I experienced the joy of running up the pitch with the ball comfortably tucked beneath my armpit. The thrill. The rush

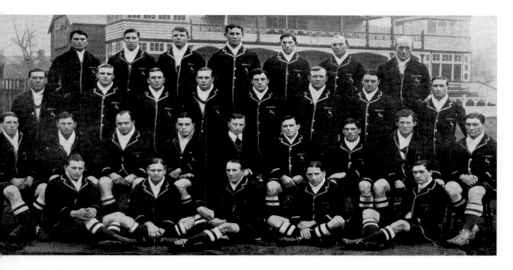

Springboks in Britain 1912–1913: A S ('Saturday') Knight, whose name I may have inherited but whose talent drifted off to other Knight kin, is in the back row, second from the left.

ALBERT ATHLETIC ASSOCIATION RUGBY FOOTBALL TEAM, 1906.

Club Rugby: The Albert Athletic Association Rugby Football Team, 1906, with WW Knight in the second row from the back, seated second from left. RA Knight is sitting immediately to his left.

Bloedwors and Galpille: The blue of Boishaai in celebratory mood. Paarl Boys' vs Paarl Gimnasium is the world's biggest schools' rugby derby, drawing up to 25,000 to the stadium on Faure Street.
(Photography courtesy Paarl Boys' High School)

'Catfish': Two old rivals square off upon the muddy fields of East London. Dale College vs Selborne is a derby epitomising the spirit of rugby in South Africa.
(Photograph courtesy Mrs M Williams)

The gallery of the Kingswood Commemoration Church, upon the pews of which Bennie Osler's name can be found.

GREY-KOLLEGE RUGBYSPAN, 1882.

Agter: J. Prior, W. J. C. Brebner, ——. Inland, Cor. Beukes. *Middel*: John Daniels,
J. Becker, J. W. G. Steyn (Kapt.), B. Bell, ——. *Voor*: Cor. v. d. Walt, J. A. Scott,
W. Robertson, J. H. Truter, ——. Snyman, C. van Bloemenstein.

Rugby takes its proud form: This photograph of a Grey College team from 1882 (note the mixture of English and Dutch surnames) shows that the traditions of rugby – evinced by the caps and long socks – were already firmly established.

Brothers in Arms: Old Grey Springboks join young Grey South African Schools boys before a test in Bloemfontein in 2009. From left to right: Piet Lindeque, Francois Steyn, Jean Cook, Ruan Pienaar, Charl Wegner, Jannie du Plessis, Stefan Kotzé, Bismarck du Plessis, Pieter Rademan, Heinrich Brüssow, Riaan Britz.
(Photograph courtesy Niel Lombaard)

Skonk: A wealth of experience and a seemingly endless supply of great stories.
(Photograph courtesy Maritzburg College)

A sprightly and eager pose – a certain sign of a pre-match photo. The Guys Vets XV, with Wouter standing on the far right and Iain in the back row, second from left. Kneeling on the far left is Terry and in the middle (with ball before him) is captain Pat. I am standing third from the right.

Vutha usatana! Peter Grant leads the Maritzburg College team through Nicholson's Arch and onto Goldstones

Boere Oorlog: Affies (in white) vs Boys' High is a derby that always pleases the eager rugger crowds of Pretoria.

Tradition: Mascots have always played their part in South African schools' rugby. This particularly proud example wears a St Stithians jersey.

A school still standing tall, despite its early struggles: A copy of Verrocchio's David – a present from the outgoing headmaster, Reverend John Nash – stands defiant in the David Quadrangle of St John's College, Houghton. (Photograph courtesy St John's College)

of adrenaline. Heart pumping. And then I was thumped to the ground.

Play continued as I picked myself up, Tony using his experience (he has been playing for the club since 1978) to harass and disrupt the opposing backline, and Duncan making a thundering run up the field. But as the game wore on Lowestoft scored two late tries. With minutes remaining, we were forced to be ambitious, so the forwards began passing the ball, while the fly half furiously waved his hands about and shouted out numerous codes to indicate that we may actually have some set moves.

I was at the bottom of a ruck – my face planted firmly in the mud and some half-naked strangers scattered over me – when the referee signaled the end of the game. The 80 minutes of organised thuggery that had gone before was quickly forgotten as my exhausted teammates formed a tunnel to clap the victorious Lowestoft team off the pitch. Then, after they had reciprocated, both teams headed for the communal showers and a cold pint in the club bar.

It was absolutely brilliant. I loved the gladiatorial unity – sweating and bleeding for a common cause – of a game that accommodates all shapes and sizes. And even as I collected the corner flags and scattered shapeless rugby balls, after most had left for the bar, I was still loving it. Perhaps it's the game's Corinthian spirit and its old stoic values. Or perhaps it's simply the opportunity to legally klap some strangers for an afternoon. Certainly at this level it wasn't about the money. I knew that because after showering I checked both boots for any misplaced notes that may have been slipped into them.[78]

Despite the amateur game still adhering to many of its traditions, the professional version has had its inevitable effect. The days of tours and other old traditions have become remarkably blurry. However, professionalism, for all its faults,

---

[78] The common method of payment in the amateur days, or so I'm told.

also ended much of the hypocrisy that had always dogged the amateur game and it also sorted out the problem of who foots the bill for a serious injury.

The southern hemisphere's 'saviour' came in the form of Rupert Murdoch, swinging by the chandeliers and bursting through the musty boardrooms into the laps of our rugby chiefs. At an IRB meeting in Paris on 27 August 1995, just two months after the World Cup final, South Africa, New Zealand and Australia signed a 550-million-dollar deal with Murdoch's News Corporation, guaranteeing 10 consecutive years of Super Rugby and Tri-Nations. It was an exciting time. We could wake up to Waratah David Campese goose-stepping Highlanders winger Jeff 'Goldie' Wilson, and after a midday braai, tune in to see Mark Andrews stealing John Eales' line-out ball at Kings Park. With barely a week to catch your breath, the next touring team would be in the Republic.

Televised rugby saturated our screens. It was glitz and glamour; half-naked cheerleaders, fireworks, and franchises in colourful pyjama kits that seemed to change each year. And it was big money – enough money to see off the Rugby League vultures and even draw some mercenaries back to Union.

Some traditions would ultimately change. No longer were rugby players plumbers and bankers. Rugby was now their profession, and they had to serve their home union and the television set for 11 months each year. More so the latter, as even the administrators themselves had to dance to Murdoch's tune – renegotiated deals, more money, new franchises, different

Super formats, et cetera. South Africa took the largest slice of the revenue pie because most folk left their TV on the SuperSport channel while they braaied, though soon games and scores merged into one another so that the only thing most of us could recall about the previous year's Super tournament was that 'that one damn Kiwi side won the thing *again*'.

From sneaky pre-professional professionalism (or shamateurism), to enormous revenues in pounds, euros and yen, the game has changed at a giddy rate. It is perhaps what makes the coming Lions tour so remarkable. Yes, the players are getting a bit more than a social allowance, but it's built on the foundation of a traditional amateur tour.

Consider the original Lions tour to New Zealand and Australia. The players had to sign affidavits on their return affirming that none had received any money whatsoever. The early Lions also had to pay 80 pounds up front to cover their spending money on tour and their dinner jacket. As many could not afford that, their clubs back in their villages and valleys had to step in and assist.

Forty years later things had changed very little, and the Scottish Rugby Union insisted that each of their Lions players return the two blazers, playing kit and grey flannel trousers which they had been given before their five-month tour of Australia and New Zealand in 1966.[79]

Even on the 1993 tour of New Zealand, when Lions bigwig Bob Weighill asked for an extra pat of butter to accompany his hotel breakfast, he was told he didn't qualify for extra-butter privileges.

'Do you know who I am?' asked Weighill, before giving the waiter his full title.

When he had finished, the waiter looked at him. 'And do you know who I am?' he asked Weighill.

'No,' replied the Englishman.

'I'm the man in charge of the butter.'[80]

Though I had come to an understanding early on in my rugby career that I would never play at any great level, and certainly not at a level where folk would actually *pay* to watch me, I was

---

[79] Richard Bath, *The British & Irish Lions Miscellany*, p. 72. They sailed from Southampton on 11 April and travelled to New Zealand by passenger boat via the Panama Canal, arriving in Wellington on 17 May.

[80] Richard Bath, *The British & Irish Lions Miscellany*, p. 3.

nevertheless wholeheartedly enjoying my sojourn in English club rugby. The season had worn on and despite my average debut I had become a regular in the Thurston Second XV.

On a fresh October afternoon, we, the Thurston Seconds, found ourselves huddled in a ring for warmth, and perhaps even some sage advice before the game, which was now only minutes away. Duncan tried to fire us up, reminding us that we must start putting what we had practiced on the training ground into effect in our matches – this despite the fact that Duncan and I were the only players from the Seconds who actually attended practice. His speech ended with a few foul words that seemed to get a positive response from Phil, the flanker. Looking over his shoulder to where the Cantabrians Club were gently passing a ball to each other, Phil hissed a timely reminder of the previous year's away game against them. Each dirty tactic that Phil threw out (whether true or absolute bollocks) brought down a hail of curses from our tight five. Finally, Duncan deemed the side suitably fired up, and we dispersed for the kick-off.

As fate would have it, the kick-off went hideously wrong, and the ball was unintentionally torpedoed along the ground, scooting past our pack and bobbling toward our try line. I collected it as their wing closed in, my teammates leaving me with no uncertainty as to my only available option: 'Kick! Kick! Kick!' they chorused.

I decided to run.

My instinctive plan was a swerve to the left followed by a big step to my right, but instead it became more of a crab-like shimmy followed by a stumble. And it was in that moment that I discovered what it must feel like to be one of those cursed rugby professionals whose rational thought escapes them at a critical moment in the game. The Cantabrian winger had little trouble in catching me and soon bodies were enthusiastically piling up on top of me. Moments later the ref's whistle blared for a penalty against me. 'Killing the ball,' he muttered.

Thankfully, my contribution to the game improved after that, largely due to our forwards, who gained the ascendancy through sheer intimidation. Thurston is by and large a farming community, and thus fortunate to have a seemingly inexhaustible supply of podgy, less-than-pretty front-rowers who are always fantastic sledgers.

Our back row, led by Duncan and Phil, were also playing another blinder, and fulfilling their loose-forward mandate admirably: the opposition were thumped (mainly off the ball) and any protruding limbs at the ruck (mainly theirs) were stood upon with great vigour.

With our pack going forward, we were even ambitious enough to pass it beyond Keith at fly half, and before the first half was over I had scored twice. The first came through an overlap that began in our own half, and swept upfield with every player barring the puffing front-row contributing. It ended with me bellyflopping over the line with the ball. I didn't break into song – Basil Bey would have frowned upon that – but instead jogged back, chuffed at scoring a try after a drought of at least 10 years. The second try came from a mucked-up set move, but as the ball bobbled into my mitts, I sidestepped the defence and dotted down beneath the sticks.

Thurston went on to win the game handsomely and it wasn't long before we were heading for the communal showers.

It's always a wise thing to be first to applaud your opponents through a tunnel after the game, as when they reciprocate you can keep trotting on happily towards the showers to enjoy the limited supply of warm water. From the change rooms – a small, unkempt concrete block – it's to the bar in traditional club tie and jacket, for a warm spud and a cold pint.[81]

A great club spirit exists in England and I had enjoyed my time with the Thurston team. However, by the time November

---

[81] This is merely a temporary measure prior to returning home and putting a pack of frozen peas on all the aches and bruises.

arrived it was time for me to move on. My unashamed excuse for leaving Keith and the team was 'country over club'. I had bought tickets to all of the Springbok matches on their year-end tour of Britain. It would be a month of trials for all involved as the locals and the Boks strove to solidify their positions for the looming Lions tour.

SWING LOW

Since the heady days of English dominance in 2003, the six major European rugby nations have played 76 Tests against the Tri-Nations sides. They have won 13 (and of those five were French victories). Be it hosting June internationals or touring at the year-end, the Tri-Nations sides have been infinitely more successful than their rivals in the northern hemisphere. However, the Autumn internationals were a wonderful opportunity for the British and Irish teams to regain some pride and prepare for the looming Lions series.

Who'll be President? Obama vs McCain ... that was tame. Now for the battle that will really get our pulses racing – Habana vs Our Shane! a headline on a copy of the *Western Mail* screamed. I had joined what seemed like half the South African diaspora on a train from Paddington to Cardiff for the early November Test.[82]

The beauty of train travel to Cardiff is that you're deposited on the doorstep of the Millenium Stadium, and after a short

---

[82] *Western Mail*, Saturday 8 November 2008.

walk through 'chippy alley' I arrived at the finest stadium in world rugby.

Wales is a true rugby land, more so than any of the other 'home nations'. Though it wasn't that long ago that Welsh legend Gareth Davies was famously quoted as saying, 'We've lost seven of our last eight matches. The only team we've beaten was Western Samoa. Good job we didn't play the whole of Samoa!' Welsh rugby has enjoyed something of a renaissance in recent times and though they have yet to return to the glory years of the 1970s they have certainly escaped the recent decades of mediocrity. The valleys are singing once more. In fact, Welsh voices in unison – especially the haunting 'Land of My Fathers' – is something every rugby fan must one day hear for themselves. The French have the rousing 'La Marseillaise' and Argentina the passionate 'Himno Nacional Argentino', which inevitably brings the front row to tears every time they belt it out, but the sound of the Welsh voices that filled the stadium as I searched for my seat will forever be one of my most memorable experiences at a rugby match.

When the game did start, however, it was the Bok fans that were making the noise. Two tries, one of them a Jean de Villiers intercept, and two penalties pushed the Boks to a comfortable 20-3 lead, and barring the large, straw-haired Andy Powell, who was a particular menace, the Bokke looked to be cruising to victory – rookie fly half Ruan Pienaar giving a mature display of tactical kicking.

However, the Boks were made to sweat for the win in the closing stages. Wave after wave of Welsh attacks resulted in a number of penalties and Wales edged closer, willed on by the red masses below the echoing and enclosed dome. But despite a man in the bin, the World Champions saw off the fiery challenge of the Grand Slam Champions and the spoils of the first tour game went to the men in green.

FINAL SCORE:

Wales	15
South Africa	20

The next game was in cold Edinburgh and so I headed north towards the land that gave us bagpipes and Bill McLaren.

Gothic Edinburgh is an impressive city, albeit lacking the rugby fever I had witnessed in Cardiff a few days earlier – Princes Street was largely devoid of navy Scottish rugby jerseys that Saturday morning or anything really to indicate the Scots would be at war in a matter of hours. Perhaps the painted Bravehearts were all lying in wait at the stadium.

Murrayfield – resembling some of the older South African stadiums (Kings Park and Newlands) and perhaps pushing its sell-by date – was icy, and a chill wind swept across the pitch. As if in response to these typically Scottish conditions it was the home team that came out firing, and scored their first try in 14 months! They went on to prove that they can be a wily lot and by half-time they led 10-0. The Boks seemed fatigued, uninterested, impotent. Surely we could not lose to this lot! A Welsh journalist once said: 'Getting beaten by Scotland is like getting mugged by the Brownies.' It would be daylight robbery to lose to the nation who must have insisted on Italy's inclusion in the old Five Nations to ensure they were no longer bringing up the rear.

The Boks, bless their fashionably late souls, scored 14 unanswered points in the second half – three Pienaar penalties and a try by Jacques Fourie – before holding out against a ferocious finish by Scotland to take their second victory on the road.

FINAL SCORE:

Scotland	10
South Africa	14

The final game was against the English at Twickenham. On the preceding Thursday night I attended a Lions Legends event at Lords Cricket Ground. A 'press conference' had been arranged beforehand, though there were only two other journalists. JPR Williams was first up, and as we arranged ourselves around the great fullback, we introduced ourselves and our professional allegiances with journalistic courtesy:

First British journalist: 'British and Irish Lions official website.'
Second British journalist: *'Daily Telegraph.'*
Me: 'Personal.'

Which, after a moment's hesitation from JPR, was probably interpreted as: Just here for a laugh, really.

This end-of-year tour was in many ways a curtain-raiser for the forthcoming Lions series. The hype around the Lions tour was already building momentum and these Tests were an opportunity for the locals to gauge their chances of winning a Lions series and for the players to cement a place in the squad.

'I'm glad to hear that the tour is returning to its traditional roots – that they'll be "sharing rooms" and not "sleeping together" as one paper quoted me as saying,' stocky JPR began. 'South Africa is very hospitable,' he continued, 'off the field!'

Jeremy Guscott arrived a few minutes later to offer his thoughts. 'Borthwick is the obvious choice as captain. He gets his place irrespective,' he stated when asked about captaincy. 'Every Lions tour is a near impossibility,' he said a few minutes later. 'The odds are so stacked against them. In 1997 we wanted to prove Louis Luyt wrong. He had publicly written us off, so it served as a real motivation.'

Willie John MacBride was last up. The man whom every journo wants to hear from when it comes to Lions matters, he is the epitome of humility and, like Morné du Plessis, a man who commands the utmost respect in world rugby. 'The captain

135

needs to be a man of stature,' the large Irishman responded when I asked him to give us his thoughts on who should captain the team. 'He needs to have the respect of the opposition.' Then, looking at each of us, he said, 'You guys don't understand the importance of the media – it can destroy a tour or a team.'

Although it didn't make sense to me then it was something would ring true by early July 2009.

Securing a ticket for a game at Twickenham is about as likely as a Freedom Front rally in a township. It's an almost exclusive club for the old-boy blazer brigade to meet up and have a yarn. I only had a ticket through membership at the Thurston Rugby Club and because they'd have loved me to be around when they gave 'us' a hiding.

South Western Trains were my transport to Twickenham, and upon it I met Namibian 'Wurm' and his girlfriend, Sandra. Wurm was kitted out in genuine antelope antlers and his makeshift cape was a Springbok skin draped over his back.

We disembarked at Twickenham Train Station and followed the masses through Twickenham suburbia to rugby's HQ.

So, to the game. With a hearty version of 'God Save the Queen' out of the way, the match announcer tried to stem the mood in the stadium by requesting 'no booing' when the opposition took their kicks, followed by a reminder of the respectful ethos of the game. But, as it turned out, the Poms could have been forgiven for some loutish behaviour. A record score was soon racked up by the Boks as they brought England's sweet chariot to a shuddering halt. It rained points, including a dazzling first-phase try that began at the line-out, lacerated the English midfield and ended with Adi Jacobs crashing over the whitewash. But perhaps Bok power, pace and purpose was epitomised in one tryless moment. With about 20 minutes to go and the Boks in a 30-6 lead, English flyer Paul Sackey surged upfield, the try line beckoning and the roaring crowd willing England on. But the galloping 'Bakkies' Botha had an alternative ending in mind. Sweeping across the field he launched his lighthouse frame at the winger, bundling him into touch. Moans erupted around the South East Stand where I sat smugly. 'Whose idea was this?' someone groaned behind me. 'Hopefully South Africa will leave the pitch early so we can score a try,' another muttered. 'But even then you can't be sure with our lot.'

Despite a repeated call to end the jeering, coach Martin Johnson's livid mug on the big screen only encouraged a torrent of abuse. The white flag was raised long before the end, and as the second half wore on Twickenham's 81,113 grew as porous as the home team's defence.

At 70 pounds a ticket this game was one of the most expensive I had ever attended, but as I watched the Boks on their lap of honour I decided that it had been well worth the money. I clenched my fist like Schalk Burger below me as the Boks marched and from the field to a deserved Christmas break.

FINAL SCORE:

England	6
South Africa	42

Why the seemingly immense gap between the two hemispheres? Is it 'Too many sweatbands; not enough sweat,' as Colin Meads once surmised? Or is it, according to Stephen Jones, the doyen of English rugby journalism, simply that, '*They* want it more.'[83] Certainly, it was a warning to McGeechan and the Lions. But then the shrewd Scot is a different creature, unperturbed by

---

[83] Stephen Jones, *Sunday Times*, 30 November 2008. In the *Theory of Modern Rugby* (p. XV) by I M B Stuart, Stuart bemoans the fact that the English provided most of the world's games and yet lack the ability to win: 'We wonder why it is that other countries can defeat us at most sports, and the answer is to be found, not in that they are physically more endowed than we are, but that they have the temperament to practice doggedly their weakness, and endeavour to improve before they proceed any further. The Englishman, on the other hand, refuses to identify his weakness and practice assiduously to correct it [...] He refuses to practice, what he calls "drudge work", except now and then.'

underdog status, and with a healthy respect for the Lions jersey and its traditions, and if he were to lead the Lions to a series win in South Africa it wouldn't be the first time he had achieved rugby glory against all the odds.

MEETING MARTIN

Not far from Thurston is the ancient town of Bury St Edmunds. The final resting place of Mary Tudor and Kind Edmund – the unfortunate victim of Vikings' arrows in 870 – Bury St Edmunds has seen more than its fair share of history. For the avid rugby fan, however, it is Bury Rugby Club that will be of most interest, and it was the club's strong youth programme that coaxed England coach, Martin Johnson, out of London for the day a few days after the debacle at Twickenham.

Johnson accomplished the near-impossible feat of captaining the Lions to glory in South Africa in 1997, and as the Boks' attention would now be firmly focused on the Lions series, I was eager to get his thoughts on the coming tour.

The club was a hive of activity of young aspirants and proud parents when I arrived. On the B Field, Martin Johnson, in navy blue RFU tracksuit, towered above his admirers, who eagerly soaked up any advice he was prepared to part with. However, as Johnson was whisked off for 'photos' (with the legion of children and their coaching staff) it became increasingly clear that the day's proceedings were hastily being wrapped up and that Johnson was eager to get back to London, probably for a Premiership fixture. With no other option I followed him into the club's dank corridors beneath the small Pavilion stand and cornered him in the only place I knew I was certain to get a word in – the toilets.

Johnson was hunched awkwardly over a urinal more suited to a 12-year-old, his huge frame stooped below a poorly placed light fitting. I introduced myself, and he didn't seem too perturbed about my chosen venue for the interview. Perhaps, though, the last thing he wished to hear after the heavy defeat only days earlier to the Boks was another South African accent, but I fired away regardless: 'Martin, who's your choice of captain for the Lions tour?'

The Lions had already chosen their management. The next question was who the all-important captain would be. Johnson is right up there with the finest of Lions captains (being the only player to have ever captained two Lions tours), so if there was a man with a pedigree to respond to my question, it was Martin Johnson.

Unfortunately, his response was typical of those who have fended off one too many journalists in their time: 'It would have to be someone senior and respected by his peers,' he muttered.

And that was it. The rest of my questions were met with the words 'You can contact me through the RFU'.

This was not the first time my efforts at interviewing a player or a coach had been met with resistance, and I certainly didn't blame Martin for not wanting to talk to me – despite my best 'I'm not a journalist' efforts, I still come across as one. I was merely content to see the humorous side of the day: I doubt the 2003 World Cup-winning captain has ever been interviewed in a more obscure setting.

GUY'S HOSPITAL

Wintry December had set in as I started my new teaching job. Exchanging the countryside of Suffolk for bustling London, I'd taken up a position at Bickley Park School, a feeder school for the likes of nearby Dulwich College.[84] I've always thought that sport, and especially team sport, is helpful for any (manly) young man, and at Bickley Park I'd be spending a good portion of the day teaching nine-year-old boys that the aim of the rugby is to take the ball forward by passing it backwards. You can see why many of the world's finest coaches cut their coaching teeth at schools level: To get the *attention* of young boys is an achievement in itself. To get them to *understand* you is an even more amazing feat. But to get them, in an hour of practice, to actually *transfer* this knowledge into what they do on the pitch is near impossible and has driven many a fine young coach to madness. I have learnt – the hard way – that schoolboys ought not to receive more than two or three instructions at a time. And even then it needs to be succinct, *contra* former Hurricanes coach Colin Cooper, who once said at practice: 'You guys line up alphabetically by height and you guys pair up in groups of three, then line up in a circle.'

At Bickley I stumbled upon another social team, through Pat Gush, a Welshman and my Head of English. This time, however, the team was the pinnacle of rugby amateurism: the veterans team of the world's oldest rugby club, Guy's Hospital,

---

[84] In recent years Dulwich have produced players like Andrew Sheridan and Nick Easter (whose great-grandfather Pieter le Roux played for the Springboks).

established 1843.[85] I have no medical background and was yet to turn 30, so how I qualified for the 'vets' team of a hospital was beyond me, but it was rugby nonetheless.[86]

A vets rugby team, I was to discover, is an altogether different beast, so different in fact that some have even questioned whether such a team can be classified as playing rugby. By definition a vets team implies that a full team is never guaranteed. When 15 players do pitch up, it may be that 11 are forwards and the rest are backs. A last-minute position shuffle could easily leave a team with a lock at scrum half and a prop on the wing. The age restriction for such a team is officially anyone over 35, though the average age probably hovers around 45. They certainly boast an abundance of experience, and this alone makes them lethal to unsuspecting opposition as they are the masters of the old-school tricks and probably invented a number themselves. Terry, our 65-year-old hooker, has nearly six decades of learning how to 'assist' the ref and get up the noses of the opposition. Picture Sean Fitzpatrick – just a bit wrinklier – but with twice as much streetwise cockiness. A devastating asset to any side.

Even back in the 1870s when the game was still taking shape, some delightful tactics were being instilled. W G Gray, the captain of Guy's Hospital, wore a sleeveless jersey against St Thomas' in a cup match so that he could put 'a modicum of oil on his bare arms to make it difficult for his opponents to catch

---

[85] Some years ago the Labour government realised that it was too expensive to have so many separate medical schools in London, so they rationalised them into groups. Guy's, St Thomas' and King's are now one teaching school. The Inter-Hospital Challenge Cup was a prominent series of games in the English rugby calendar, and it still exists.

[86] Interestingly, Guy's is a club with a rich South African heritage. One of the biggest English clubs in its early days, and responsible for the modern three-quarters line, Guy's has always attracted medical students from England's numerous former colonies. In the 1918-19 season, South African Doherty captained an all-South African team littered with Van Schalkwijks and Van Niekerks. In fact, South African representation came to a head the following year when England's fullback was dropped for South African W J Olivier.

hold of him.'[87]

My 'veterinary' call-up came within a few weeks of me starting work at Bickley. It was under clear skies on the banks of the Thames in south-west London that I played my first game for the club against Harlequins RFC vets. 'Be there and ready at 13:15 for the 14:15 kick-off,' Pat had told me. Most arrived at 14:00 (my first vets lesson and the game had not even begun). Of those who did finally pitch up that cold afternoon, two spoke in a dull, homely South African accent. Iain, a regte Boer (and wearing a Blue Bulls cap to prove it), was a flanker who organised tours to South Africa when he should be teaching at the local school. Wouter, from Strand, had been in exile long enough to begin a young family, and had played inside centre for a number of years for Guy's. We were a rather cosmopolitan side, really: a Kiwi, a few Welshmen and a Greek all arrived in the club's navy-and-gold hoops.

The game was minutes away, so some kind of a non-strenuous warm-up had to be done. A bit of touch rugby ensued, and a minute later Pat called the team together for a spirited team talk: 'Lads, let's do some interesting passes and other strange things.'

Harlequins were doing equally strange things.

'Wat maak hulle?'[88] Iain asked bemusedly of the opposition, who seemed to be warming up with a run around the field. Such strenuous exercise is frowned upon by most veteran teams. Training and pre-match warm-ups are anathema. The theory

---

[87] TLT Lewis, 'A History of Guy's Hospital Rugby Football Club', in *Rugby Club 125th Anniversary, Guy's Hospital Gazette*, p. 585. The game, however, seemed to have varied results for him, as this extract confirms: 'Unfortunately, he dislocated his shoulder early in the second half. He retired to the pavilion, but when three members of the Guy's staff failed to reduce it, he returned to the field and played fullback. Later, under chloroform, the reduction was quickly accomplished but the triumphant ride back to the hospital, in a "growler" with the coveted Cup, was marred to some extent through the vomiting induced by the anaesthetic.'

[88] 'What are they up to?'

being that enough of these things have been done.[89]

This wasn't an epic fixture likely to draw a swelling crowd, and my wife had wisely opted to 'let me enjoy this one on my own'. Perhaps she had heard the sage words of the late Virginia Graham, who once said of rugby: 'The women sit, getting colder and colder, on a seat getting harder and harder, watching oafs getting muddier and muddier.'

And so, on a typically grey and cold afternoon, 30 oafs prepared for rugby and mud.

Early in the game, a great scoring opportunity went begging. With Harlequins on the attack in our 22, Wouter (pronounced *Wooh-tah* by his English teammates) knocked on in attempting to intercept a floating pass. Had he caught the ball cleanly he may well have gone on to score, but there was relief on his face when he returned for the ensuing scrum. 'That would have been a long way to run,' he said.

Unfortunately, we spilt a few more opportunities that could have yielded tries, and whether our line-out calls were 'Nigerian gold' or 'Johnny's underpants', the ball always seemed to fly directly to the Quins stand-off. I don't think we won a single line-out.

The rucks were a mad, lawless frenzy, and in the interest of self-preservation, I avoided them as much as I could. But we had more luck when we swung the ball among the backs, who seemed a good deal quicker (and less grey) than the Harlequins lot. But a try always eluded us. Perhaps it was our sheer lack of fitness … or practice … or a warm-up. Or that most of us were ruck

---

[89] There are some wonderful stories down the years to prove this point, but none more apt than that of Dickie Lloyd. In 1914 he was selected for Ireland to take on the Welsh in Belfast. Following a pre-match team photo, he thought it wise to embark on a gentle jog around the pitch before the game kicked off. A fatal mistake. He pulled something and had to watch the entire game from the stands. He should have listened to his forefathers, who 40 years earlier (before a game against the English) had claimed to be 'immaculately innocent of training'. Ireland, of course, were thumped that day, but it's a mantra that still carries weight with most veteran teams.

inspectors when dogged, gritty scavengers were needed.

But I had little excuse late in the game. Breaking clear of the Harlequins centres and metres from the try line, there was only their cross-covering left wing to prevent me trotting beneath the goal posts. I could have put my head down and with the instincts of Habana launched myself at the line. I didn't. Instead I passed to Pat and Wouter who were both haring up on my inside. Exactly who the ball was for, I wasn't quite certain. Nor were they, and the ball was fumbled a metre from the line.

By the final whistle, I was exhausted. My throat was dry, my cheeks burning, which was no consolation considering we had snatched defeat from the jaws of victory.

FINAL SCORE:
Guy's Hospital RUFC Vets   11
Harlequins RUFC Vets   13

Despite the near-freezing conditions, Wouter departed with Iain to get his traditional Saturday (and *every* day for that matter) braai fired up. The rest of us headed for the Harlequins pub to enjoy a warm meal and a pint, and sing a few merry songs that reminded our hosts that although they had beaten us, we were still older than them.

SARRIES AND SEFFRICANS

The lure of the pound, euro and yen has seen a brawn drain of talent from South Africa in the professional rugby era. Most look to the French leagues and by April 2009 the highest influx of foreigners into the French Top 14 came from South Africa.[90] 40 per cent of all players in that league were in fact foreigners, the number growing all the time. Many more Saffas lurk in the leagues below that as well, a great number of them without any professional experience in South Africa, but for whom a contract with a French club is their chance to enjoy some pro rugby.

The English Premiership also hosts numerous forgotten Boks and men who toiled in Super Rugby for years. Most Clubs have a Botha, a Venter or some other familiar pilgrim loitering within their kraal.[91] However, of late the British press has been putting the boot into Saracens Rugby Club, who they claim have recently been murmuring in far too distinct a South African taal. Saracens have had a history of South African influence in the professional era, beginning with Francois Pienaar's player/coach role. But a recent takeover by an influential South African group (SAIL) has put the cat among the pigeons. Johann Rupert's core business is Richemont, but his involvement with sport dates back to the United Tobacco Company sponsoring soccer in the 60s and Dunhill's lucrative sponsorship of golf. He was also involved in arranging non-racial cricket in the 70s and

---

[90] 33 professionals in the highest league. The French clubs have no salary caps and the British clubs thus struggle to match them financially.

[91] Even Grey High old boy Mike Catt still trudges on as a player/coach at London Irish. Alongside him is coach Neal Hatley. The old Dalian only recently retired after 263 appearances, a record at the time. Apparently the burly prop proved he was worthy of a contract each year by bench-pressing more than any of his younger challengers.

personally funded the Dan Qeqe Stadium that I had visited in Itembilihle. So, when he was approached by the then English-owned Saracens, he was only too happy to consider furthering his already substantial investment in rugby. Changes, however, would have to take place at the struggling club. The door was shown to some players and, disgruntled by the upheaval, coach Eddie Jones resigned. Brendan Venter was appointed as his successor, his third stint in the Premiership, and he joined the growing number of his countrymen at the club. Rumours of top-flight Boks being brought in to replace those who had departed and speculation that Saracens may try and move itself closer to the large ex-pat community in London added to the general anxiety that an old club was being slowly turned into a Super 14 franchise.

I met Edward Griffiths – recently appointed by Saracens as Group Chief Executive – on the 15th floor of the St George's Hotel, in its quiet restaurant with views over central London. The blond-haired administrator is a familiar face to many, having been the Chief Executive of South African Rugby during the '95 World Cup and in the immediate aftermath of rugby turning professional, before falling out of favour with the dictatorial Louis Luyt.

Edward was already there, and rose from his cappuccino to greet me. Wearing an open-collared shirt and with a backpack at his feet, he was a laid-back presence in such a bustling city. Born in Rhodesia, Griffiths was raised in England. After his education, he headed south again. That was in 1985 and on a day when Province beat Northern Transvaal at Newlands to win the Currie Cup. By the age of 26 he was the Sports Editor at the *Sunday Times*, from where he would make his way to Chief Executive of South African Rugby. An exhaustingly impressive CV also includes working on South African bids for the 2004 Olympics, the FIFA World Cup 2006 and 2010 and the Rugby World Cup 2011. He was also Head of Sport at SABC, the founding chairman of the South African Rugby Players Association and the author of 22 books. In June last year, he seized the opportunity to join Premier Team Holdings, and with it the daunting task of growing the Saracens brand.

'Our aim now,' Edward began, 'is to establish a commercially viable cub that builds upon the existing supporter base but also attracts international support, including the resident South Africans.'

Despite the large interest in the game and the financial stability of England's RFU, the game is littered with its own challenges.

'English rugby is a very difficult environment,' Edward explained. 'For instance, it is very difficult to make money here if you don't hold ownership of a stadium. There is also a negativity and apathy among English supporters; many are resistant to change.'

Changing the subject, I pushed Edward for his thoughts on the game's progression 15 years on from the beginning of professionalism.

'The people involved with the game still sense the deep amateur roots running through it,' Edward stated. 'Take the example of injuries. In football, a player may be injured, and his contract terminated shortly thereafter. He will move onto another club quite easily, and perhaps many more clubs after that. It is the norm. But in rugby, if this happened people would be aghast. "It's not in the spirit of the game," they would say. "How can a club do that to one of its own?" Rugby still has that sense of friends getting together for the good of the game and having a beer afterwards.

'So the sport is at an interesting stage, still holding on to some aspects from the amateur era,' he continued. 'However, even in such amateurish traditions as the Barbarians games and Lions series, there are many people making substantial amounts of money. For instance, the Barbarians may ask a club to release one of their players for a game. The club may think it a great thing to keep going and good for the game, because of all its traditions embedded in rugby, et cetera, but consider that a top player earns 200,000 pounds a year. Before releasing him, his club might think, "Hold on, he'll be playing for the Barabians in a stadium in front of 60,000 people, at say 50 pounds a head. So, the gate-takings become three million pounds. Say 500,000 pounds for the ground and expenses, and someone's making a lot of money from a bloke I'm paying! So why should I release him?" But people would be up in arms if you refused to release a player. They'd say it was against the spirit of the game!'

I spoke to Edward about a few more of the current issues in modern-day rugby. Regarding the allegations of the 'Africanisation' of Saracens, he simply said, 'When the dust has settled, it will hardly be the "revolution" that many have made it out to be.'

And what of Saracens' Premiership ambitions?

'It is not the big names that will win the season for you,' he told me. 'Most are only available for half a season anyway. A Premiership team is successful because of the characters upon which it is built. Building a successful team and support base, including providing a place where South Africans can meet, is imperative to our club.'

I descended in the lift with as calm and collected a man you are likely to see in rugby's administrative corridors. If he is anything to go by, then Saracens is a club on track for plenty of success.

LEARNING FROM THE WISE

The vets rugby calendar is not like that of those silly boys who play Super Rugby, Currie Cup and Springbok rugby – all in one season! If they could only see what they're missing out on, they would instantly move across to vets rugby. A game a month is about as hectic as it gets, and even that's not guaranteed. Half of the fixtures are cancelled as many of the players are not keen on the thought of overexerting themselves. Various factors need to be considered, especially if it's an away game to another part of London. *Train lag* and *acclimatisation* come into play, and sometimes even the dreaded *altitude factor* if they are to play a game in north London.

The season, however, had trudged on, and I'd punctually arrived for another game, this time at our home ground in the heart of Surrey. Although it was now late February – and there were only two months remaining of the rugby season – I knew that this may very well be my last game for the vets.

Wouter and Iain arrived together. Both were kitted out in London Irish tracksuits, and thinking that they were just using a typical vets ploy (establishing the early 'I'm an ex-pro' psychological advantage over your opponents) I didn't think too much of it. However, I found out later that Iain was the cousin to ex-Bulls and now Exiles hooker Danie Coetzee, and thus he happily received any surplus stock from Danie's cupboard.

It's never been the expectation of a non-First XV club side to field the correct number of players. Sometimes there may be a surplus of up to 10 substitutes offering fresh but aged legs, but more often than not numbers are lacking. That Saturday things were no different, and despite the fact that Pat had sent out an e-mail to just about every post-World War II Guy's player and also encouraged some of the doctors to bring along any recovering and able patients, we took to the field resembling (in numbers at least) a Rugby League side.

Although a lack of numbers is a minor issue in vets rugby, it does create problems. For a start, most players soon begin suffering from 'Positional Alzheimer's'. Your original position is soon forgotten as you end up covering anything and everything from hooker to fullback. It could even be argued that amateur rugby players are more versatile than the so-called 'utility backs' that professional rugby likes to boast of.[92] In professional rugby, such players acquire this tag because they have the 'ability' to play a position that would otherwise be a few metres from their more accustomed position. When a forward unwittingly wanders off to the backline in the professional version of the game, he is rebuked and threatened with castration if he does not make a hasty return. In vets rugby he would be applauded for such imagination.

Our opponents that day were Dorking Vets, and after winning the toss Pat opted to play downhill in the first half. This was not only an immediate advantage but a decision that would also bear fruit later in the game as, though we would be playing up the hill in the second half, it was likely to be at least 10 minutes shorter than the first half. Rarely will a vets player complain about this, and if he does, the exhausted ref will have none of it.

We took to the field to one or two cheers from a lone spectator. Most of us wandered about aimlessly, unsure of what exact

[92] I'm sure at some stage many professional rugby players could have been classed as true utility backs, but only when they were amateur players. The towering Springbok lock Bakkies Botha played a number of school years as a centre before professional rugby crippled his versatility. He was a true utility back then. I, for one, would love to see him removed from the entangling scrum and thrown out into the centres, where he could be given the ball and released like a galloping giraffe on the open plains. So too was Os du Randt an eighth man before being sentenced to the front row. He complained bitterly to his coach at the time (prior to Craven Week) but by the end of the week, he was singing all the way to the South African Schools team.

position we were playing or ought to be filling, before readying ourselves for the kick-off.

The whistle blew to get things underway, and the usual din of advice – directed at the referee – and insults – directed at the opposition – soon began (and that was just from our supporter). With our lack of numbers, we had had to effectively sacrifice our wing positions, and Pat told me to hover at the back, and 'use my discretion' when it came to positional play.

Moments later the ball was hoofed down the centre of the pitch and I collected it on our halfway line. There is rarely much of a follow up, so I decided to head east for the sidelines. The Dorking No. 11, who may just have been the slowest winger in all of England, approached. I swerved past his well-rounded paunch, drew the cover defence toward me, and slipped the ball back to Terry (who had been waiting on their 22) and he scrambled into the corner for a try.

Shortly thereafter, a slick backline movement – that may have even brought a tear to a Springbok's eyes (had any one of them been present) – ended with a beautiful inside pass to Wouter, who bisected the Dorking halfbacks and surged beneath the poles. More amazing was the fact that it had been rehearsed before the game.

After his try, Wouter retired to the sidelines for a deserved break – more than acceptable in vets rugby.

With a few more dubious tries awarded and our opponents tiring and retiring, Guy's moved into a handsome lead. Then the ref muttered something about five minutes remaining in the game, although I was sure we'd only played about 15 minutes of the second half. But there were few complaints.

FINAL SCORE:

Guy's Hospital RUFC Vets:	41
Dorking RUFC Vets:	22

As it turned out, the game against Dorking did end up being one of my last games for the season. A couple of tours followed – to Cardiff and Italy – though I'd be lying if I said these revolved around rugby. The season petered out and of the four fixtures remaining, only one transpired. The log at the end of the season made for some interesting and confusing analysis.[93] Few teams had played the same amount of games, and it also seemed that some teams had improved on their position after consecutive losses. But that would not be out of order in a vets league either.

TEAM	Played	W	L	D	For	Against	Diff	Pts
London Welsh Vets	10	8	2	0	303	138	165	44
Old Paulines Vets	9	6	3	0	274	156	118	42
Harlequins Amateurs Vets	10	4	6	0	135	260	-125	36
Old Cranleighans Vets	10	3	7	0	218	253	-35	34
Wimbledon Vets	11	3	7	1	191	345	-154	33
Guy's Hospital Vets	7	5	2	0	150	139	11	32
Dorking Vets	9	1	8	0	75	305	-230	24
Met Police Vets 2	3	1	1	1	50	85	-35	9

My foray into club rugby – with both Thurston and Guy's Vets – had shown me that amateur rugby was alive and kicking in England and had taught me that the best thing about being a part of a club was the camaraderie. At this level the very essence of the game is the people who play it. It all had me wondering what the South African administrators were doing to keep club

---

[93] This list has been shortened for the sake of page space and to make our final log standing appear better than it really was.

rugby afloat. What were they doing to protect the foundation of the game in South Africa? How were they encouraging fresh-faced school-leavers to continue with the game?

VI

KINGDOMS, REPUBLICS AND EMPIRES

The big derby

June 2009

Mid-May 2009 and the Super 14 final had come and gone – the rampant Bulls reclaiming their crown – and the Six Nations had reached its tumultuous conclusion – the Irish reclaiming the title with their first Grand Slam in 61 years. However, both of these things felt like a curtain-raiser to the series of the year: the British and Irish Lions tour to South Africa.

I arrived back in South Africa on a flight congested with red jerseys; a Barmy Army of travelling Lions support – 30,000 had been expected to follow the tour. With the first Test a week away, I'd be picking up my journey around South Africa in KwaZulu-Natal, beginning in the Midlands and from there on to Durban. I'd be meeting some of the game's most committed rugby people, sampling stories from some of KwaZulu-Natal's finest rugby schools, and, in between, trusting that the Boks would come right in their greatest Test since 2007.

SKONK

In Pietermaritzburg, the historic capital of KwaZulu-Natal, is one of South Africa's finest rugby nurseries: Maritzburg College.[94] One man in particular has been instrumental in growing the school's fierce rugby reputation that over the years has had many an opponent packing spare underwear in his tog bag. James Mervyn Nicholson may be his name, but he is known the world over as 'Skonk'. Raised on a farm in the Underberg, he grew up more fluent in Zulu than English, something that worried his mother enough to sentence him to boarding at Durban's DHS. It was there that he got his nickname: Future head boy M C F Bennett thought Nicholson's stamina on the athletics track was akin to a strong ox on his farm, which went by the name of Skonkwan. In Zulu it literally means 'peg', as in a strong and dependable tent peg that is capable of doing its job. Inevitably, the school's Zulu staff referred to him as iSkonkwa though to the boys he remained Skonk. According to the man himself the staff were great supporters of the DHS First XV and of Blackman House (the boarders' First XV) in particular – especially during interhouse rugby. On Fridays they would dish up meatballs for the boarders' dinner and the story goes that to give them additional taste, and some 'extra rugby vitamins', the cook formed all the ingredients into a ball by squeezing them under his substantial armpit. This was to ensure the First XV team would play with

158

---

[94] John Scott, the Lieutenant-Governor of the Colony of Natal at the time, wished to establish two secondary schools in the colony – one in Pietermaritzburg and one in Durban – which had no schools at the time. He offered the councils in each town a deal whereby if they raised the 5,000 pounds needed to build the school, the government would give them land to the value of 6,000 pounds on which to build it (large sums of money at the time). The result was Maritzburg College, which was founded in 1863.

more 'man fire' (satana). However, in retrospect it does also shed light on the day boys' perception of boarding cuisine.

After his World War II service in 1944, Skonk was sent off by the Natal Department of Education to Maritzburg College for six months. Sixty-four years on he's still there and still coaching! Perhaps then, the name 'Skonk' was well chosen. However, the strange nickname has not always been mastered by those ignorant of the Zulu tongue. In 1960 a touring team played College and after the game both teams enjoyed supper in the Victoria Hall. After an introductory speech by Wally Sharrat, it was the turn of the tourists' captain to respond. With the hall in respectful silence, he began his opening address: 'Mr Headmaster, *Skunk Nicholson* ...' He got no further until the roaring laughter abated. In an effort to correct what he thought must have been a slip of the tongue, he began again: 'Mr Headmaster, *Nick Skunkolson* ...' And that was it. The boys doubled over, the speech was forgotton and the red-faced captain stood perplexed, fumbling for the words to correct himself.

Nevertheless, the name Skonk is now synonymous with rugby excellence. I am not aware of anyone who has ever coached as many teams as Skonk has. Danie Craven used him to coach as far away as Chile. He was also a South African Schools selector and coach. And when South Africa sent a multiracial under-18 team to Wales, Skonk was the coach. He has coached club sides, including Collegians and DHS Old Boys of Durban, and has even helped out with the Natal senior team. Overall, he has serviced eight rugby boards and unions, 13 rugby clubs and 41 schools (spread over five countries). Even in 2008, at 91 years of age, he was still assisting with the College seventh team, or mSataans. And at the end of the year, the boys insisted he join the team in their rugby photo.

Skonk's impressive First XV record with College stands at[95]:

played: 504
won: 403
drawn: 49
lost: 52

Fifteen of his teams were unbeaten in Natal with 10 of them unbeaten against all-comers. Of his boys, Keith Oxlee, Ormie Taylor, Andy van der Watt, Joel Stransky and Jeremy Thomson played for South Africa. Over 60 players who went through his hands played for Natal. Nearly 200 players played for Natal Schools.

It is a rugby CV surpassed by few. But what I have most enjoyed whenever we've met is how his old face lights up each time a name comes to mind. He'll inevitably shift to the edge of his seat and some priceless anecdote will emerge.[96]

Arriving at the red-bricked Maritzburg College, where I had arranged to meet Skonk, one of the first things you see is the small, unused sentry box just inside the school gates. It was once mistaken for a long drop, so Skonk had a plaque put up, explaining its more important military purpose during the Anglo-Boer War. Just beyond it is the venerable Victoria Hall, upon which a Red Cross flag flew during that war. Today, it is a national monument, and within it are the names of the College boys whose lives were lost during war.

After parking, I made my way towards the foyer, an entrance similar to so many traditional schools – the walls are lined with immaculate oak honours and achievements boards, stacked with the names of boys who have excelled academically or at sport.

A few minutes later Skonk arrived, accompanied by his

---

[95] Skonk coached the First XV until 1982.

[96] It is said that of the estimated 8,630 boys who have been privileged enough to enjoy his tutelage, he has rarely forgotten a name or face.

daughter, Diana. His lanky flanker's frame is now hunched and even though our last meeting had only been a year earlier, he looked decidedly older.

Most will remember Skonk cutting a lone figure, seated upon his shooting stick behind the try line with binoculars in hand – no doubt analysing his boys and the opposition from below his worn farm hat. He held an uncanny ability to recognise the opposition's strengths and to neutralise them, to find their weaknesses and to capitalise on them. I had heard more than once how difficult it was to defeat a College First XV but to do so twice in a season was well-nigh impossible because Skonk would have devised a counter to whatever methods had been employed to beat his team the first time around. Like all masterful coaches, Skonk could get the best out of every single player on the pitch, often conjuring successful positional switches from the sidelines, but his teams were perhaps best known for their aggressive go-forward philosophy. This was epitomised at the coin toss, where Skonk taught College captains that when they chose sides their response should be: 'We'll *attack* those posts'.

As we made our way from the school down the slope to the rugby fields, Skonk, once described by Ian MacIntosh as the 'Doc Craven of Natal rugby', began to enlighten me on the history of Goldstones, the battleground that is the main rugby field at College.

The length of field nearest the school is known as Basher Ridge because of the 1,400 College boys, with straw bashers upon their noggins, who are seated there on game days. There used to be jacarandas that shaded the boys and which occasionally clung to bashers that had been exuberantly tossed up – the tradition every time the College First XV score a try – Skonk recalled. Basher-tossing was a common sight, especially in the Nicholson years. From 1948 until 1980, College lost only seven times at home. Skonk turned Goldstones into a graveyard for visiting teams.

The field itself is more sun-baked, winter-dried earthworm

cast than it is grass, and you could swear the feather beds of Hilton and Michaelhouse – situated on estates either side of Pietermaritzburg – are in an altogether different solar system. Bruises are inevitable here and it always seemed that the sneering locals took great delight in this fact. Even as early as 1906, the great Bill Payn, as a College schoolboy, was once stopped from removing hardened worm casts from the rugby field before a game with Michaelhouse.[97] 'Don't throw them all away, you silly buffer,' an irritated peer rebuked him. 'Leave some for the visitors!'

As we stood surveying the hallowed turf I asked Skonk what sage advice he left ringing in the boys' ears as they emerged from the change rooms at 100mph. It wasn't long before he was passionately shouting out Zulu phrases, telling me that this was the only way to use the terms:

'Faka emgodeni!' – *Put him in a hole* (ie make it difficult for him).
'Shaya pansi!' – *Tackle hard/scrum with great power*.
'Ngiyom hlutha!' – Used by a prop: *Take the feathers off your opposing prop* (ie show him no mercy).
'Vutha usatana!' – *Play with more fire*.
'Soba gobisa!' – *We will bend them in the scrum*.
'Liya shona ilanga!' – *The sun is setting* (ie time is running out).
'Isinswa zabo bathambile!' – *Their players are soft*.

'There are many ways of motivating boys,' Skonk said, 'but these Zulu words have to be passionately spoken for emphasis!' He then let rip with another spirited dose of Zulu.

College, having educated Keith Oxlee, Joel Stransky, Butch James and Peter Grant, could claim to be one of the finest fly

---

[97] The days (before 'staff' were employed) when the boys themselves had to prepare the fields.

half factories in world rugby.[98] And there is no question that this has a lot to do with Skonk's unusual coaching techniques. Having exhausted his collection of Zulu war cries, Skonk told me a story from his early coaching days about a courageous young scrum half by the name of 'Stumbles'. To improve his skills, Skonk had shifted him to the Second XV during practice so that he could play behind a pack that struggled more than its First XV counterpart. There Stumbles would be forced to deal with slow ball from his forwards and so develop vital scrum-half instincts and skills. However, in a practice match the Seconds were heaved back so powerfully that Stumbles, true to his name, fell and disappeared beneath 16 pairs of studded boots. Skonk gave a shrill blast on his whistle to end the play before his star scrum half was injured. Once the dust had settled and the packs had disentangled themselves, Stumbles was left on the ground moaning and clutching at his groin. He rose in great pain and his shorts had to be lowered for an inspection of the damage. Plenty of fresh blood oozed from various lacerations in and around his manhood, and he was quickly removed to the tap – the great saviour for all rugby injuries. Then, when the bleeding was under control, Skonk ordered Stumbles into his car so that he could take him to the sister at the sick bay. Stumbles recoiled in horror, and blurted out: 'I would rather die than do that, sir!' The suggestion seemed just the remedy, and by the next practice he was back, this time behind the First XV scrum.

College boys can be a superstitious lot, who love ritual and ceremony. Never is this more evident than on Reunion Day. Leading up to this day and most other derbies, there is much heroic talk of 'blood' and 'honour', amidst cries of 'Faka emgodeni!' and 'Vutha usatana!' On the Friday night before late roll-call, the boarders, with a few day boys thrown in for good measure, will gather in the old Clark House quadrangle for the

---

[98] Perhaps only Christchurch Boys' could compete with that record. Their recent alumni include Andrew Merhtens, Aaron Mauger and Daniel Carter.

sacred boot-blacking ceremony. All College boys, from the lowly second former in the u14Gs to the exalted skipper of the First XV, are required to play in black boots (no matter how much their fancy coloured footwear may have cost). The senior boys will be sitting on the stoep, their feet in the gutter, as they polish their boots and swap old war stories in hushed voices. Later, they will make their way down to the rugby fields for the sacred 'flick' – that much-cherished but rather dubious ritual of puffing on a cigarette before flicking it over the poles. With the call of 'Jimalayo-Ji', a final war cry ensues in the darkness before the boys traipse off to bed.

The matches themselves are emotional affairs, and the open teams have a wonderful tradition on Old Boys' Day in which all the matric boys are allowed to run on first, to be followed later by the juniors. Each boy is to clutch his hand over his heart as he runs onto the pitch and whenever a kick is being taken at the poles. College teacher and old boy Matthew Marwick once explained the reunion of Old Collegians to me as 'the gathering of Highland Clansmen in the build-up to the slaughter of the Sassenachs'. You could swear war never left this region though Brit, Boer and Zulu no longer battle for control over land, but for possession of an old leather ball and the chance to stick it over their opponents' try line.[99]

Skonk then began to pull out some of his more treasured memories:

Brian 'Toffee' Sharp, the goal kicker for the first team from 1962-64, aroused much interest in Natal with his kicking. Known as the 'round-the-corner kick' by his contemporaries, it is now used by almost every kicker in the modern game, but it

164

---

[99] In fact, the colours of College's jersey reflect the warring history of the region: black for the Zulus, white for the British and Boers and red for the blood which flowed. The College badge continues the theme – an assegai and a rifle meeting.

had fallen out of favour by the mid-60s.[100] At the beginning of the '61 season Sharp was having problems, so Skonk sent him down to Snows Ground to spend some time improving his place kicking. Later, when Skonk went down to the ground, he found Toffee was having real success with his round-the-corner kicking. Naturally, Skonk encouraged him to spend time on this type of kicking as he had become amazingly accurate with it. In a match against Glenwood in Durban in 1963, Toffee decided to kick for the posts after College had been awarded a penalty on the halfway line. Mr Pat Mungavin, the Natal referee in charge of the game, had never seen this type of kicking before, and thought that Toffee was about to kick at the wrong posts. He was however suitably impressed when the kick bisected the uprights perfectly. Toffee Sharp's kicking was copied very successfully by many College boys and it soon became the only way of place-kicking in South Africa and, of course, elsewhere.

'Spade' de Graaf was the No. 8 in the great College side of 1978. However, prior to an away game at DHS, as the school bus was preparing to leave, Skonk noticed that Spade looked rather unwell. On enquiring what the matter was, Spade told him that he was very worried about having to play against the great Michael Barker, the DHS and South African Schools No. 8. The coach assured him that he had nothing to worry about and that the College pack would put the DHS pack on the back foot, and so nullify Barker. However, his reassuring words had little effect. Finally, 'Swazi' Meyer, a powerful and aggressive prop, said that he had some herbal tablets that would calm De Graaf down. Skonk immediately ordered the prop to fetch the tablets from his dormitory. Skonk gave De Graaf one tablet before the bus left for DHS, one when they arrived, and another one about

165

---

[100] It was way back in the 1930s when a boy by the name of Colin 'Foxy' Forsyth from Glenwood High School amazed everyone when he used this style of kicking. However, for some reason it fell out of use in the early years of World War II and all kickers reverted to the straight run-up, the toe of the boot being used to make the kick.

30 minutes before kick-off. The tablets seemed to work and De Graaf played a blinder of a game, scoring three tries to the one scored by Barker, and helping College to a resounding 19-12 victory. On the way back to Maritzburg College, Skonk asked Meyer about his pills. The prop informed him that he got them from the pharmacy to assist him with his acne!

College boys would seem to not only possess refined rugby skills but also quick tongues. Udu Koch, a boarder inclined to regular bunking, was one such example. He had regularly inquired of Skonk how he could build up his upper body to become a better winger. One evening, Skonk had spent a late night at Clark House preparing exam papers with another master. It should be also be mentioned that the boarding house has an ingenious way of getting boys out of the first-floor dormitories in case of an emergency. Each dorm holds a long, thick rope that is bolted into a wall near the window. This rope can be thrown out of the window for boys to abseil down if a hasty escape is needed. As Skonk left the House just before midnight, his car lights came upon the figure of Udu Koch dangling halfway down Clarke House on an escape rope. He pulled over, and asked him what he was up to. Udu's quick reply was: "Sir, you have advised me to build up my upper body strength so I am doing some exercises on the rope."

Skonk then spoke of great wins on Goldstones, of the early days of the game (when it took two days by scotch-cart to travel to nearby Greytown), and of Peter Nel hitting the wing of a Welsh u20 side so hard 'it made the Queen jump 10 feet in Buckingham Palace'. However, many of Skonk's most cherished memories from his time as a coach have little to do with rugby. For instance, when Australia arrived in South Africa for a cricket Test in the midst of apartheid, Skonk and fellow coach Ronnie Chambers decided to attend. They were sitting in the baking sun and decided to nip across to an adjoining section and find some shade. They were happily seated on the grass until a police constable came by. 'Oi,' he shouted, 'can't you read? This section is only for the coloureds.'

The cricket was momentarily forgotten as all eyes fell upon Skonk and Ronnie.

Ronnie was of a rather darkish complexion, and promptly told the constable that he was indeed coloured, a response that was met with warm applause.

'And you?' the constable said to the pale Skonk. 'You're not coloured!'

Skonk replied: 'No, I'm not, but I married his sister, so I've been reclassified!'

The constable grunted, mumbled something inaudible, and carried on.

Of the 28 teams that College are capable of fielding on any given Saturday, there are bound to be some who wish to enjoy the game from a different perspective. Craig Joubert, College old boy and now renowned international referee, arrived at Goldstones to join us. He had learnt his trade on this very field, and I was keen to get the referee's perspective before night fell upon Pietermaritzburg and my time with Skonk was over.

THE SACROSANT REFEREE

It is widely but not universally acknowledged that the referee is the most important man on the pitch, although it sometimes seems to be that it is the ref himself who spends much of the game ensuring that everyone knows this. This was clear from rugby's very first international. It was a game between Scotland and England and it took place in Edinburgh in March 1871. Whether the English had forgotten the rules agreed upon before the game, or were just caught unawares, the sneaky Scots had driven over the try line and declared that a try had been scored before the away side had had time to gather their wits about them. The English protested bitterly. The referee pondered. The try was awarded. Later, the referee explained the decision in a letter: 'I do not know whether the decision was correct. When an umpire is in doubt, he is justified in deciding *against* the side which makes most noise. They are probably in the wrong.'[101]

1885 was a historic year for rugby: referees were given that blessed (and equally cursed) whistle. However, it was only allowed to be blown if the umpire (today's touch judge) raised his stick (today's flag, albeit on the end of a stick). Before the introduction of referees, outcomes and disputes were settled by the opposing captains, and it was only in 1892 that referees were finally given sovereign control of a match. If the law happened to be repealed, I would quite fancy John Smit debating on behalf of the Boks. It would be great to have the beefy front rower squaring up to tall Paul O'Connell as they debated Law 117.2(a) regarding who may or may not be responsible for the umpteenth collapsed scrum.

Apart from the lousy pay and the health risks associated with telling 30 large, angry men what to do, refereeing is a fulfilling job – or so Craig Joubert seemed to be arguing as I listened to him and Skonk exchange some banter. Craig was tall, dark and – contrary to my ref preconceptions – young. However, at only 31 years of age, he had built up a staggering international CV over the previous eight seasons. I glanced at the sheet Craig had

---

[101] Sports journalist Peter Corrigan once wisely said: 'Players and spectators at all levels can enjoy sport better if they totally accept two simple rules. Rule one: the referee is always right. Rule two: in the event of the referee being obviously wrong, rule one applies.'

mailed me of all the travel he had undertaken since turning pro in 2002. It listed 19 countries and a total of 75 international trips. In 2007 Craig had spent 212 nights away from home, of which 171 were overseas. That year, to ensure some stability, he proposed to SARFU in 2007 that he be based in Australia during the Super 14. In any given year referees usually travel to Australia/New Zealand four times during the Super 14. As referees were expected to arrive in a country on the Sunday before the game, Craig's deal ensured less jet lag and a home in Brisbane for four months each year.

I asked Craig about some of the great games he had presided over, and why he was mad enough to turn this much-abused hobby into a profession.

'Schoolboy rugby is very close to my heart. I started refereeing as a schoolboy at Maritzburg College, where rugby is a religion, and spent the first four years of my career refereeing only schoolboy rugby,' he said. 'Maritzburg College has a history of producing referees and the late Ian Rogers was the pioneer in this regard. He was encouraged by Skonk to take up the whistle and became the top referee in South Africa. He refereed at the '95 World Cup, but passed away in 1998 after being diagnosed with cancer after a game in Australia.

'I was really encouraged by my late dad, himself a provincial referee, to take it up and together we spent many hours refereeing schoolboy rugby, invariably with me taking charge of the curtain raiser, or Second XV game, before he refereed the main game,' he continued. 'Maritzburg College was extremely good to me in this regard, and through my years there I progressed from refereeing the u13Es and Fs to the high-profile Saturday afternoon games on Goldstones before large crowds.'

'And the comparison in intensity between schools and professional rugby?' I asked.

'Not too much of a difference, really,' Craig replied. 'The ferocity and passion in schools rugby is not dissimilar to that seen in Test matches! Large crowds gather to watch the traditional derbies and while the great stadiums I have refereed in, like Stade de France, Twickenham and Eden Park, are amazing, with crowds of up to 80,000 people, the atmosphere I've experienced on Goldstones or at Hilton College on derby day is every bit as electric. It's almost like a mini-Twickenham with up to 12,000 people crammed in. In fact, the atmosphere is probably even more electric as the crowds are so much closer to the field than in the great stadiums.'

'And your favourite derby to referee?'

'Ah, there are quite a few good ones, but the three that stand out for me, based on personal experience, are Hilton vs Michaelhouse, Maritzburg College vs Grey College and Maritzburg College vs DHS. These games draw big crowds, have a festive atmosphere and a history of tough, uncompromising and often spectacular rugby. They are still among the most enjoyable and demanding fixtures I have ever refereed.'

As fine a bloke and referee as Craig Joubert is, it is a given fact that the referee can never win. An immaculate and sinless performance will always leave half a stadium (usually the ignorant half) disgruntled and displeased with the ref. Unfortunately, it seems to be at the grassroots level where you are most likely to bump into those individuals who delight in spending a long afternoon hurling abuse at the man in charge.

Craig shared the epitome of this with Skonk and I. At a derby in June 2007, Craig was asked to referee an u15A game between College and the visiting Affies. After an intense but good-spirited fixture, an incensed father approached him. With no idea of Craig's refereeing credentials, he asked him whether he knew the laws pertaining to the scrum. Craig said he knew a few. Instead of the parent explaining his version, he offered to demonstrate the laws to Craig. This ended up with the two of them 'scrumming' on the field as the parent sought to coach Craig on the intricacies of this dark art. Satisfied at the wisdom he had imparted, the parent left. He was later informed that Craig was indeed an international referee, and was in fact flying out the next day to ref the All Blacks-France game in New Zealand.

As with the players of the two rugby sides on the field, the 45th player ought not to be immune to criticism, but there are less and less referees entering the game and it's not hard to see why.[102] Impressionable youngsters are quick to learn what is 'accepted' behaviour and mimic their rasping, partisan parents. It is why, in some respects, and for the sake of the game's good traditions, the rugby ref needs to remain sacrosanct, even when sport becomes well-paid work.

The tape in my old Dictaphone had long since expired, but Craig Joubert and the legendary Skonk Nicholson were still talking. College tradition was as strong and healthy as ever, I thought as I left the two men, generations apart, sharing their thoughts on every rugby topic under the sun. It was time to move on and I had an appointment to learn the history and hear the stories of an especially treasured Midlands rivalry.

MIDLANDS MEANDER

Before accelerating along the Midlands Meander, towards the Nottingham Road Brewery, you would be advised to spend some

---

[102] And perhaps it would be quite refreshing (and certainly a great paper headline) to hear the ref confess mistakes in the spirit of Gwyn Nicholls, who a century ago muttered after an international between England and Scotland: 'Wasn't I awful?' He was never asked to officiate another game.

time looking around the elite school of Michaelhouse.

The estate is spread over 600 hectares of rolling hills, lush bush, springs and dams, but beautiful as the surroundings may be it is the place's boarding spirit that has most recently made the headlines – captured as it is in John van de Ruit's recent *Spud* books. Entering through the black iron gates of Michaelhouse and driving down its autumnal Pin oak avenue, you pass its extensive playing fields before arriving at the ivy-clad brick buildings. The immaculate chapel, testifying to its Anglican heritage, looms over the fountain at the school's entrance, behind which double-storied buildings surround beautiful quadrangles. Within these red-brick buildings, interspersed with fountains and statues, are eight boarding houses. It is a boarding school, after all, and feels typically British. But it's now a far cry from its humble roots, when the Balgowan Estate offered no running water and electricity, and when subsistence farming was essential to supplement the boarders' diet.

Alongside Michaelhouse there is an active railway line. Transport to rugby games used to be via the train – and when the boarders arrived at the station for the Hilton game an ox wagon would continue the journey to the school.[103] That was in the 1920s and when a calendar season included five or six schools and four club sides from Durban and Pietermaritzburg (and when teachers often made up the team numbers). However, although these days almost all transport is done by bus, some things haven't changed. A sing-song is always a great way to kill time while travelling to a game. Lyrics are, as a rule it would seem, simple and generally crude. Michaelhouse boys have always been especially inclined to sing on a return trip, before crowding into their House for a warm supper.

On one Saturday evening in the 1970s, however, they were met with a rather cool reception. When the famished boys arrived, 'Numbers', the school chef, herded them into the senior dining

---

[103] Later the wagons were replaced by Model T Fords.

room, ensuring that no seat was empty. Impatient and hungry, some of the boys began taunting and threatening the pedantic chef, but Numbers would get his own back that cold winter's night. Instead of a wholesome feed, Numbers began serving boiled eggs. The roar of rage that filled the room reverberated across the quad as boys demanded a proper meal, but Numbers continued unperturbed before disappearing back into his kitchen. That was the just the ingredient required for a riot. Boiled eggs flew across the room as the boys started showing their displeasure. Soft eggs splattered against walls, tables, boys and even the chandeliers. Calm was restored only when some teachers rallied to investigate Numbers' desperate cries.

Despite the occasional bout of egg tossing, Michaelhouse is one of the country's finest schools and can boast of a proud rugby tradition. The game's ethics and purpose are instilled in the 'Cacks' and matured in its seniors.[104] The coaches are the souls responsible for this and Michaelhouse have always had some of the most passionate in the business.

At the inauguration of the Private Schools Tournament at Hilton in 1986, a crackerjack Bishops side, coached by Basil Bey, were the team to beat. Michaelhouse had run up good scores against St John's and St Stithians, but the Cape Town rugby side had comprehensively beaten Hilton and Kearsney by large margins. The final pitted the two teams against one another. During the game, a loose forward dropped the ball over the Bishops try line, a final pass to the wing was judged to be forward and a penalty hit the uprights. Plucky Michaelhouse narrowly lost 13-18, but salvaged more than a little pride for the Natal schools. Gordon 'Floyd' Paterson, their rarely pleased coach, was so overcome with emotion after the match, that he had to ask the assistant coach to step in and say some words to the boys.

173

---

[104] While Queens have Skunks, Selborne New Pots, St John's Removes, College New Farts, the fearful new adolescents of Michaelhouse are just as delicately christened 'Cacks'.

Another fine Michaelhouse coach who deserves a mention was the tall, athletic Andy 'Vinno' Vincent. In 1994, the Michaelhouse First XV were psyching themselves up in the change rooms, ready to take on Hilton in the return encounter – they had lost the first game and for most of the boys this was to be their last crack at their old Midlands rival. The aromas of Elastoplast and Deep Heat hung heavily in the claustrophobic change room, and the tear-inducing Vinno's Vapo Rub was smeared upon the faces of most.[105] Finally, the intimidating Mr Vincent entered, breaking the focused silence, and took a seat among the players. Hours of physical training and sickening sprints up and down the amphitheatre steps had all come down to this one game, and all that remained was for the coach to leave some inspirational words ringing in the boys' ears before they made their way onto the field. There was an almost sombre silence. Then Vinno rose to address his team and, as if possessed by Churchill himself, thundered the words: 'Now, gentlemen, remember the three Cs: *Courage*, *Commitment* and *Determination*!'

However, perhaps the finest pre-match foul-up occurred in 1986. It was the first game of the season for the mighty u15As and their opponents were Kearsney. As is the rule on the Meadows field, the day's entertainment would climax with the First XV game, and so a large crowd had steadily grown. The boys had begun their psyching session in the amphitheatre an hour before the game, and this had been led by one of the teachers' sons who had recently returned from the army. By the time they arrived in the change rooms they were raring to go, and when they were eventually called to take the field, the boys, in combative single file, charged eagerly down the hill that leads onto Meadows. Speeding down the steep descent and onto the field, the prop, Graeme 'Bog' Newcomb, hit the level playing field too hard and immediately lost his footing and plummeted to the ground. Enthusiastically trailing him was Charles MacDonald, who tried

174

---

[105] Tiger Balm.

to round him, but Bog decided to latch onto him in an attempt to pull himself up as he passed. Unfortunately for Charles, Bog latched onto his shorts, pulling them down to his knees and not managing to pull himself up either! The rest of the team and most of the crowd were in hysterics. The spell was broken. All the time spent psyching the team up amounted to nothing and the game ended in a tame draw.

Rugby forms an integral part of the Michaelhouse education. This begins as a young Cack, of course, when during the third session of Friday prep (not usually the most productive in the week) he is tested on his ability to recall every First XV name.[106] Should he foolishly omit any names, he is dismissed to the prefects' common room (read: intimidating cauldron for the new boy and a theatre of amusement for the tough-acting senior). After completing his lines, the unfortunate Cack will get the signature of the senior whose name he forgot. He is unlikely to forget the name again.[107]

As in all boys' schools, respect is generally earned through sporting excellence. Even fresh Cacks with some prowess on the rugby or cricket field are likely to get it slightly easier than their quivering peers. But we do tend to forget those who lurk below the all-important First XV (though this is hardly surprising considering the slippery skills slope one witnesses when watching all the open sides in their derby-day glory):

---

[106] Later in the term the whole of Michaelhouse will gather in the main quad to do the war cry at this time on a Friday afternoon. There they surround their First XV, who in turn surround the fountain more commonly known as 'Pissing Pete'. This is, it has to be said, a great time to drop a casual reminder to the cheerleaders and First XV of your mate's imminent birthday. A dunking usually ensues.

[107] The days of canings have disappeared, however one Warwick Weight – a Michaelhouse student in the mid-60s – does claim to have received the most canings in a single term: 53. Of course, this breed of student is unphased by being sent to the prefects' rooms or even receiving six of the best. They acquire a certain immunity to discipline that can be rather useful to a rugby side.

The First XV: Superheroes: huge, muscular, skilful and powerful.
The Second XV: Lesser heroes but who are within reach of the great prize.
Third to Fifth XV: Combination of good journeyman and young talent. Always worth watching.
Sixth to Seventh XV: Standards began to drift. Generally fit and keen but will never acquire any real rugby skills.
Eight XV and below: The bottom of the barrel – unfit, clumsy, two left hands. Never spoken about with any real seriousness. Their results are largely insignificant except to them.

This is not to say that attending a match involving those banished to the Eighths is not worth the effort. In fact, it can be the most rewarding and amusing rugby you could ever watch. It is *also* at this level where you will see probably the most open and expansive version of the game. This is largely because most of the boys involved are well aware that they have 14 other team mates and are quite happy to (unselfishly) shift the ball to someone else before trouble arrives. It matters little in which direction the ball is hurled just so long as it doesn't sit with you for any extended period of time. This is also a far simpler tactic than going to all the trouble of arranging a time-consuming set piece and having to remember where your head and backside need to fit into the scrum or where in the line-out you need to be lurking.

This motley gang of rugger players will include beanstalk locks; podgy, short-sighted props; some kwashiorkor-looking kid at fullback and a live-wire asthmatic wing who, if the ball happens to miraculously reach him without being dropped, will make strange adrenaline-fuelled squeals and then set off from one touchline to the other (never running straight, so that eventually his own teammates are forced to tackle him).

These are also often players with great visions of rugby grandeur. An egg-shaped prop, for instance, is very likely to opt for a delicate grubber kick with all the supposed finesse of Joel

Stransky. Of course, if he manages to put any boot polish to the leather, it is often a fine effort, and should this miracle occur and he fails to reach the ball before his opponents, he'll berate his wingers for 'not following up' and 'ruining a perfectly good try-scoring opportunity'.

These teams also consist of some of the most passionate players. They may not possess any real skill and constantly drop the ball as if it were the slipperiest bar of soap, but to hear them thunder encouragement to their unathletic teammates, no matter how many times they have glumly awaited a conversion from beneath their own poles, is always excellent value for money.

A fine captain of the Eighth XV by the name of Chris Taylor once offered me a perfect summary of what it is like to play the game at this end of the rugby spectrum: 'I never really figured out my duties,' he told me, 'but I reckoned that as captain I was required to greet the opposing skipper, make sure we had oranges at half-time, and try to ensure that all 15 bodies turned up. After the usual defeat I was supposed to ensure that we clapped the victors off the field. Of strategy and tactics I was entirely innocent. But in the Eighth XV you learned to be philosophical about it. Hell, we were always philosophical about it.'[108]

While Michaelhouse, who have an intake that is less than half the size of Maritzburg College, do punch above their weight, they also enjoy the healthy benefits that a boarding school brings to its rugby. Most fine rugby schools in South Africa have a strong boarding tradition at their very heart. Another school that has the rare distinction of being an all-boys' boarding school is Hilton College, just a short meander in the direction of Durban (and the forthcoming first Lions Test).

---

[108] Chris did his time at Tatham House from 1966-70.

LIFT UP YOUR HEARTS

Founded in a farm building with 50 boys in January 1872, today Hilton can arguably boast of one of the most beautiful school campuses in the world. Its pristine white-washed buildings look upon its 1,700-hectare estate of gorges and valleys. The school's playing fields, chapel, boarding houses and buildings are spread over the campus, giving a visitor the feeling that they are in a small, neat village. Its early farm-school days, when boys were carried up the hill by ox wagon, are now distant memories. Today, it is a flourishing, elite private school, and continues to do its bit for South African rugby. In fact, Hilton College was the cradle of rugby football in the remote colony of Natal. The black and white colours of Natal were derived from Hilton in the same way SACS gave its colours to UCT, Paul Roos gave its maroon to Stellenbosch University and the Old Diocesan Club its green to the Springboks.[109] It's also done its fair bit for Springbok rugby. As College, just around the corner, could claim to be South Africa's fly half factory, Hilton could perhaps claim to be the equivalent for loose forwards. From Gary Teichmann and Wayne Fyvie to the '94 duo of Brad Macleod-Henderson and Bob Skinstad, the Hilton coaches are clearly getting something right in the blackboard sessions on The Breakdown and Hunting the Fly Half 101.

But many new 'Poops' (that morale-boosting term for the new jittery younglings) arrive at Hilton with little or no rugby

---

[109] The First XV are the only Hilton side that don't wear the traditional black-and-white hoops. They wear an all-white jersey embroidered with the black fleur-de-lis. This coat of arms was adopted from Rugby School in England, not at all surprising if you consider that headmaster 'Cavey' Ellis, a relative of William Webb Ellis himself, was the man responsible for putting Hilton rugby on the map.

experience. This is usually true of foreigners but also of deprived boys from Johannesburg who play that game with the round ball at primary school. Such boys tend to be initially banished to the coaches of the C and D teams, who themselves, as school boys, are quite likely to have received similar rugby retrenchment, but yet remain as enthusiastic for the game of rugger as one could be. A memorable coach at Hilton in the 1980s was one 'Grass' Crossley. His nickname came from his walk; he moved as if wading through long grass. His manner of speech was that of an English colonist and he was known to rally his boys from the sidelines, spitting out his catchphrase 'Blood and guts, boys!' from the side of his mouth – this, despite the fact that his teams lost to pretty much every school in the area. Undaunted by the rarely pleasing results, the coach would be more than satisfied if one or two boys broke their collarbones or got concussed as this would mean that a severe Monday workout would be avoided on the grounds that they had gone down fighting like men.

Another interesting story is told by Matthew Fitzsimons, who, due to peer pressure, had joined the Seventh XV. In a game against Michaelhouse, he recalled a Shell/BP Scholar who had been picked for his size and not his rugby ability.[110] In fact, he had never played rugby before. However, somehow, within the first few minutes of the game, the large boy managed to get his mitts upon the ball. Facing his opponents but running backwards toward his own goal line, the ball held tightly in one hand, he launched it forward like an American Football player. Oblivious to the rules and quite content with his own spiralling throw, he only began to comprehend his mistake when most of the spectators fell to the ground laughing.

179

It is players like these that Hilton coaches – truly some of the finest around – will tediously work upon until they are polished products (or at least until they can throw the ball backwards

---

[110] Shell/BP Scholars are students from previously disadvantaged communities.

while running forwards).

The great Gary Teichmann himself was no rugby star when he arrived at Hilton. He began as a fullback in u14, was shifted to the centres in u15 and by the time he reached the First XV he had been relegated to the back row. Clearly his coaches thought him better at getting in the way down there than at the back where he had more space and time to think. At a Monday practice, after the First XV had played particularly poorly in their Saturday game and lost, Teichmann was a little worried about his place in the team, especially when the two coaches, Springbok Andy van der Watt and Klein Strydom, who were sitting on a stand nearby, called him over. This was never a good sign and often indicated that one was going to be dropped. Gary initially tried ignoring them, but they persisted in calling him. After he'd moved over to them, they began with the fateful words: 'Gary, we think you need to drop down ... to standard grade Afrikaans.' Of course, Gary Teichmann went on to greater things, captaining the Boks on a record-breaking winning streak in the late 90s, before a young, electrifying Bob Skinstad somewhat usurped him and later also took the captaincy.

Many others have made their contribution to Hilton rugby in less obvious ways. Dave Thomas, during a game in 1980, was doing his touch judge duties for the Third team on an especially cold, wet and miserable morning. The game was against DHS and near the end of the game both Dave and his DHS counterpart were behind the poles awaiting a kick. Behind them was a steep and slippery muddy decline, only a few paces from the dead-ball line. The kick was powerfully taken and came hurtling towards the poles. It missed, and was heading straight over Dave's head and down the bank behind him. In a flash of athletic genius, Dave leapt into the air and using the flag, managed to stop the ball before it descended into the dreadful abyss. The DHS touch judge, on seeing the raised flag, foolishly did the same. The goal was awarded and Hilton won by the slimmest of margins. These were the first and only points Dave ever scored for Hilton.

As is typical of all traditional boys' schools, Hilton boys enjoy a healthy respect for the traditions that have been passed down from Hiltonians before them. The fear of God is struck into all new Poops with a New Boys' Test comprised of questions which are largely based upon school history. This is perhaps the most studying any Hiltonian will ever do as the punishments dealt out by the prefects for failing are far from enticing. Every Poop transforms into an academic in those few weeks.

These new arrivals also used to be at the beck and call of the seniors. A house prefect, relaxing upon his bed, could simply holler the words 'newp' – the command that summons every new Poop in the House – and a herd of boys would stampede into his room. The last poor lad there would inevitably have some task to do, be it polishing the leather of the prefect's cadet uniform or ironing his long pants. But all Poops also had set duties that they had to perform for seniors. House fagging consisted of shoe-cleaning, blazer-brushing, ironing and bed-making, among other things. But sometimes there was a certain pride in such duties, especially when your name was Ted Keenan and your fagging duties included cleaning Mike Proctor's hallowed boots. The word 'cleaning' is perhaps a gross injustice to what really occurred. 'Boned' seems far more accurate, as it implies hours of spit and polish to bring a mirror finish to a pair of worn boots (which is not far from the truth of the matter).[111] Less prominent players' boots (locks, hookers, props) were considered a waste of time by the 'boners', but getting 'Proccie's' right boot – Adidas, according to Ted – was big news as a mirror-like toecap gave Ted the impression that somehow he was playing a vital role

---

[111] The standard procedure of prefects in charge of the boot brigade was to hold a wristwatch facing the boned surface, and if the polisher could not read the time in the reflective surface it was inadequate, requiring a fresh start and a few more hours' work.

in Proctor's memorable kicking performances.[112]

Such is the passion for rugby in the school that it takes a good deal to separate a Hilton First XV lad from a rugby field. Perhaps it is the thought of an extensive prep session. Nevertheless, during a cold, dull afternoon in 1963 – shortly before the old first-team field was bulldozed and lowered to its present level (with a pavilion thrown in for good measure) – the First XV were training. The coach, a formidable ex-front ranker with ears to prove it, owned a feisty white bull terrier called Bulla (who had pink eyes and a rather aggressive streak). There was rarely the need to encourage stragglers to 'move it' as Bulla loved nothing better than to give chase after the whistle blew and nip the heels of the nearest player. Needless to say, the team was exceptionally fit that year. However, the sky that afternoon was particularly black and threatening and there was an air of reluctance among the players as the dark storm gathered overhead – despite Bulla's presence. With a typical Midlands storm imminent, and the players trying to practice against opponents they could not see, with a ball they could not find, while avoiding a rabid dog, the breeze suddenly dropped. There was an almost deathly silence among the boys. Then, suddenly, there was a simultaneous flash of lightning and crash of thunder directly overhead. All of the boys were in the middle of the field when lightning struck the goal posts on the Falcon Oval end of Gilfillan. The posts were destroyed instantly. Rarely has a Hilton side moved so quickly as this one. The boys fled to the safety of Falcon House where, safely under cover, the First XV laughed hysterically – perhaps

---

[112] In even earlier days, however, the fagging duties for future Springboks, such as Ebbo Bastard, Clive Ulyate, Brian Pfaff and Paul Johnstone, were not quite as 'romantic'. In those days, Poops had to hand-wash socks and jockstraps.

more from shock than anything else.[113]

For most boarders in South Africa, rugby is at the epicentre of their existence. If it's not touch rugby before dinner, it's sing-song on Friday night. And it's no different for the Hilton boys. After congregating in the dining room on the eve of a big game, and following sufficient banging on tables, the pride of the school, wrapped in their white First XV scarves, are ushered in. It's a bit like the pre-Test match hype, only instead of a blarring Robbie Wessels track to welcome the Boks onto the field, the Hilton First XV are greeted by a hearty rendition of 'O Boys of Hilton' – Bob Skinstad's reworked version of 'Flower of Scotland'.[114]

One particular Friday-evening sing-song is worth hearing about. It took place in 1999, on the eve of the game against the mighty Maritzburg College. As the First XV approached the archway leading into Crookes Block they noticed that there was an unusual, eerie silence, but when the team neared the entrance to the hall the boys inside erupted, cheering loudly, and then a rousing version of 'O Boys' began. The team entered, and noticed that many of those inside looked especially emotional, with some even on the verge of tears. But the passionate atmosphere had been created not by the arrival of the First XV, but by an affable and popular senior called Gareth Armour (though everyone knew him as 'Squiffy').[115] A former College boy, Squiffy – who

---

[113] The rugby poles, at 103 feet and 106 feet respectively (it's uncertain as to why their lengths differed), were among the highest in the country. However, the incident in the 60s was not the only time the Babel-high poles received divine judgment. After Charles Yeats' fine Hilton side lost to Michaelhouse in the early 70s, the school was in a state of mourning at dinner that evening. As if hearing their anguish, a violent thunderstorm arrived and shook the school that night. Some swore that God was showing his disapproval at the result. The next morning the rugby posts lay in pieces on the field, felled by the lightning the previous night. At Hilton, it would seem, lightening does strike twice.

[114] Skinstad would later reinvent the Stormers brand, replacing the original kit – which bore an uncanny resemblance to a clown's pyjamas – with an all-black strip and introducing the *Men in Black* theme song in the late 90s.

[115] Because, despite his tender years, he had apparently already broken his nose five times.

was to start for the Second XV the following day against his old school – had made a quick speech shortly before the First XV had entered. The humble farm boy, by no means renowned for his oratory skill, had stood up on a chair at main table wearing his old College rugby jersey, inducing a stunned hush in the hall. When finally he had the attention of all 500 boys, he'd said quietly, 'I've bled and sweated for this jersey!' There was a long pause. Then, taking the jersey off, he revealed his Hilton Second XV jersey. 'But that's *nothing* compared to how proud I am to wear this jersey,' he finished. The entire dining hall erupted.[116]

Before the Hilton boys are sent to bed on Friday night, house prefects inspect every bed for hospital corners, and black and brown shoes must be polished. Untidy beds or clothes not in the locker can result in an overturned bed and all your clothes thrown out of the cupboard.

It's an early start the following morning. The whole school gathers on Gilfillan to sing the school song. At six am! That's as tough a tradition as you will come across. At the breakfast that follows, boys take up seats at their respective tables with a prefect at the head of each. He'll help himself to the fresh egg and bacon, before passing it down to the rest of the boys. However, before bellies are filled, grace is said:

Prefect: 'The earth is the Lord's ...'
All: 'And the fullness thereof.'

---

[116] Hilton boys had long tried to gain a psychological advantage over the ferocious College boys and Squiffy's contribution was to be the start of a special weekend. He scored in his own game and then watched Hilton beat College for the first time on Goldstones for decades. The school mobbed their team at the final whistle, delighted at what had been achieved. Tragically, Squiffy died in a car accident in January 2001, but those who knew him and saw him play rugby remember his passion and humble nature.

And after the meal:

Prefect: 'Lift up your hearts ...'
All: 'Unto the Lord.'

Like most traditions, this has also changed over time, and there have been occasions when the closing grace has been said first. On one occasion, the hungry boys were awaiting grace when a bench fell over with a loud crash. Fungi, the designated master on duty, said, 'Lift up that bench!' To which the whole school responded, 'Unto the Lord!' And then everyone sat down to devour their food before Fungi could do a thing about it.

Although these days breakfasts at Hilton are the stuff of legend, meals there have not always been to the boys' satisfaction. In fact, the poor standard of the food and a lack of respect for their headmaster at the time once led to outright mutiny.

In 1953 every senior boy and even a few from Falcon House, the first-year dormitory, walked out, leaving behind them a few uncommitted school prefects and some ignorant first years. The rebellion had begun in the dining hall. When the master on dinner duty had arrived all the boys present had stood up and started shouting, stamping their feet and lifting the wooden tables in disgust at the food they were being served. Finally, having made their point abundantly clear, the ringleaders led their peers down the road and off the school property while the helpless master looked on.

As the evening wore on most of the boys made themselves comfortable in the forests that lay towards Hilton Road, while negotiations between the unpopular headmaster and the boys' representatives took their course. Eventually, having been promised that their grievances would be addressed if they returned to school, the boys drifted back to school in small groups. However, there never was any further debate. Instead, the chairman of the board of governors arrived at the school, and after his meeting with the headmaster the whole school was advised that each boy would be flogged, beginning with the ringleaders and matrics – something that took the best part of a day, with all the masters taking it in turns.

But the headmaster hadn't counted on the story making international news. Somehow stories of what was going on at the school turned up in newspapers in New York and London and it wasn't long before parents were arriving in droves to find out what had happened to their sons. The headmaster resigned at the end of that year and the food improved substantially.

Shortly after Saturday breakfast, the fields of Hilton College come alive with active young boys all out to impress their coach, parents and the St Anne's girls. These days up to 8,000 folk can easily be expected on Gilfillan when Hilton College play the red-and-white 'thick stripes' of Michaelhouse. Parents and old boys arrive in the Midlands from all corners of the country (and the world), and it's not uncommon to hear of some Joburg parents flying in by helicopter. It is in almost every way a particularly grand occasion. Blankets and camping chairs annex land beside the First XV field while Michaelhouse moms wearing red-and-white scarves trot past the black-and-white gazebos put up by the Hilton families. Boerie rolls are *out*. Roast beef, prawn sandwiches and champagne in crystal are *in*. Then, finally, as the early-morning mists rise, some kind of hybrid mix of a summer concert at Kirstenbosch Gardens and a gladiatorial spectacle unfolds.

OLD CROCS

Passing sugar-cane plantations and rolling hills, the N3 descends from the Midlands and heads for historic Durban.[117] However, I would first make the briefest of visits to Botha's Hill on the outskirts of Durban before pushing on to the Lions Test.

Botha's Hill is home to the famous Kearsney College. Nestled within a leafy suburb, Kearsney was first established in 1921 in the house of sugar baron Sir Leige Hulett, but soon moved to its current position to avoid the malarial mosquitoes that plagued its original site. From there, after overcoming the mandatory early hurdles like a dearth of suitable fields, leanings toward soccer and the lack of local opposition, rugby at the school flourished and it wasn't long before one of South Africa's oldest rugby traditions, dating back to 1931, was begun. It is known as the Old Crocs game, and involves a season-ending match between the First XV and a group of provincial and Springbok players of yesteryear. It's always a good-natured occasion – the whole school lining the fields to cheer on their peers against a group of renowned vets. The competitive spirit of the game draws numerous rugger-buggers back each year. Of course, there are many stories from Old Crocs games, but perhaps the one that encapsulates the spirit of these encounters better than any other is that of Wally and Owen Clarkson.

Wally Clarkson had broken his collar bone when tackling his

---

[117] Today, Pinetown, Westville and Durban are all part of the eThekwini Municipality. The area was already known as iTheku when the first white settlers arrived, though where the name originally came from is unclear. According to some, it derives from a bloke in the Lethuli clan under Chief Shadwa, who upon gazing over the oval bay that would later develop into Durban promptly declared that the area would be known as iTeku or 'the testicle'.

opposite number in 1941, and on strict instructions from his wife and doctor was forbidden to play for the Old Crocs again. In 1949 his son Owen was in the first team, but despite his desire to join the game Wally was to be found sitting quietly in a chair on the side of the field in his Springbok blazer, patiently awaiting the kick-off. However, it was at this point that Alf Walker, himself a Springbok, came across and told Wally that one of the team had not arrived and asked if he would consider playing.

Wally said that it would be difficult as he had no kit and would have to overcome the protestations of his wife. Alf replied that they could overcome the former by borrowing kit from the boys, but that he would have to sort out the latter. Wally told his wife that he could not let the side take the field with only 14 men, honour was at stake, and after much wrangling she reluctantly agreed. Ten minutes later Wally ran onto the field resplendent in a borrowed green-and-gold jersey, much to the delight of the crowd, and later in the game he had the satisfaction of going over the line to score, his son Owen hanging on to his old man in vain.[118]

The reward for the victorious side in these games is a humble mug that has been painted silver, but although the trophy might not be the most valuable the game still becomes tense when the scores are close. And when you're a ballie playing against the likes of Matt Stevens and Brad Barritt, the lost art of mauling becomes especially important to keep the ball away from your younger opponents. John Allan, CEO of the South African Rugby Legends (that now organises the event), once told me that they won the game against Barritt's slick team through a rolling maul that started in their own 22 and ended up under the Kearsney poles. 'Even Dick Muir couldn't miss that conversion kick,' he said.

188

---

[118] In those earlier games the Old Crocs played in their international and provincial jerseys.

According to Allan, the on-field, non-negotiable rules of the Old Crocs are:

1. If you kick the ball, you chase it.
2. If you chip the ball, you'd better collect it.
3. If you drop the ball, you get replaced.

But the most important part of Old Crocs games is getting together afterwards to catch up with old friends and relive the war stories – although, even while having drinks, old rugby values remain (meaning that, for at least the first hour after the game, the forwards will only drink with the forwards and the backs with the backs). 'Every time we meet for a drink after the Old Crocs game I'm always reminded of Gerhard Harding's glass eye,' Allen told me. 'During one game against Eastern Transvaal, we were thumping them when the stadium lights went out near half-time. But they shortly came back on, to which Gerhard muttered: "Ek is so bly. For a moment I thought I had lost sight in my other eye as well."'

For Allan, the purpose of the annual Old Crocs game is to encourage boys to keep playing the game after school. This is where most of the work of the company (which though endorsed by SARFU maintains its Section 21 status and thus its independence) is done: at rugby's grassroots. From coaching the coaches to the Adopt-A-School programme (where a top school works beside a less fortunate one to raise their standards) and the Iqhawe Programme (that aims to put talented youths who would otherwise not have the chance to play into a secondary Craven Week – in theory, taking disadvantaged children, teaching them life skills and finally giving them the opportunity to play in a rugby festival), this is tangible rugby development.

THE FIRST LIONS TEST
(20 JUNE 2009)

And so, finally, to the first Test. Beside the old Kings Park a new stadium is emerging for the 2010 FIFA World Cup. It will be remarkable when complete, but although it will loom over its outdated brother it will lack the history and memories that make Kings Park the venue it is. And not all of these are painless, for it was in Durban where the Lions wrapped up the series in stunning style (with Jeremy Guscott, that strutting peacock, nailing the coffin closed with a drop goal). And this after the *Cape Argus*, having reported on the Lions' early games against the provincial sides in that '97 series, boldly declared: 'The Lions look like Pussycats'. The first Test was snapped up by the hungry Lions, and the expected comeback in the second Test never materialised. The out-of-sorts Boks won the third Test but by then the series had been lost and the Lions after-party was a week old.

Guscott may have written his name into Lions folklore after securing the series with his drop goal, but it was that accursed flaming-haired Welshman, Neil Jenkins, who refused to miss a kick throughout.[119] Which is even more incredible considering his arm was still weighed down with a six-inch metal plate, inserted after he had broken it against England earlier that year. The wily Ian McGeechan did the rest, picking six ex-League boys, including Scott Gibbs, Allan Bateman, John Bentley and Alan Tate. A master stroke as they had no inferiority complex when facing the world champs, and as the tour took place in the

190

---

[119] Jenkins kicked 41 points in the three Tests, and in doing so broke the record for most points scored by a Lion in a Test series.

early days of professional Rugby Union they added a physical League element that the Boks struggled to counter.

But the Springboks are a shrewder lot this time. They're settled. They've not discarded the experienced players that brought them their second World Cup. But most of all, they're highly motivated to exact some revenge for lost pride. They're hungry to make history.

It was a red-and-green carnival outside, dare I say it, the *ABSA* Stadium. Music blared. Drink flowed. And the inviting smell of braaing steak drifted across the assembled masses. For the touring Lions supporter, it must have been an altogether unique rugby experience – shorts and shirts were the order under Durban's warm winter sun.

After the South African anthem had been blurted out, the Test began in frenetic fashion: the Boks pumping Smit through a soft defence in the early minutes and earning two penalties thereafter. Beast strangled Vickery in the front row, Matfield soared in the line-outs and Pienaar and Steyn returned the Lions to their own half with the thump of leather boots upon the leather ball.

The Lions flair flared at times, their centres punching holes through the Bok midfield. However, the Boks, despite weeks of little or no match practice, did not look undercooked, as had been feared. And yet after 50 min and holding a 26-7 lead, we could have been mistaken for thinking that our coaches had also purchased the Adidas Lions jersey – a rugby jersey the company says will sell more this year than any of the other major English Premiership teams they sponsor. Like an over-enthusiastic chef unleashed upon a perfectly good stew, new ingredients were thrown into the mix until it was difficult to imagine how it originally tasted. The dominant scrum was reduced to impotency when that fine fetcher, Brüssow, 'man-of-the-match' Beast and Captain 'cool-as-a-cucumber' Smit were replaced. But even then the itching coaches were not satisfied and Ruan Pienaar, Fourie du Preez and Bakkies Botha – all of whom had played critical roles in establishing the Bok lead – were also substituted.

Only committed, scrambling defence saw the Boks home. In fact, beyond their three tries, the Lions crossed the chalk another four times but failed to score. The series was alive and well and thus far it was worth waiting for.

FINAL SCORE:

Springboks	26
British and Irish Lions	21

I would stay on in Durban for a few more days as I still hoped to get to two old rugby schools before shifting inland to the highveld and the next Test.

GRASSHOPPERS AND HORSEFLIES

Nicknames are a part of rugby's fine tradition. When Pretoria's team was called Northern Transvaal, Louis Schmidt was referred to in a cartoon as the 'Blue Bull'. Not only is the team now known as the Blue Bulls, but the union is known as the Blue Bulls Rugby Union. Cape Town and Stellenbosch universities are referred to as the 'Ikeys' and the 'Maties', and although both names were originally used to mock those who played for the other side the nicknames are now treasured.[120]

The two great rugby schools of Durban, Durban High School (DHS) and Glenwood also have fine nicknames for each other.[121] DHS, who may refer to themselves as 'School', are 'Horseflies' according to Glenwood. DHS, in turn, call Glenwood 'Grasshoppers'.[122] The origins of the nicknames are rather blurry but one explanation seems the most likely. In the years between the wars, many of the properties on the Berea near DHS still had stables and wherever there are horses there are horseflies. A similar problem existed at Glenwood, only they were plagued by locusts. The locusts, or grasshoppers, had markings that were similar to the colours of the Glenwood rugby jersey, and so Glenwood was christened after the pest.[123]

Rugby games against your neighbours are always intense and spirited. DHS boys used to especially enjoy drowning out their arch-enemy's war cry. That cry would end with the spelling of Glenwood: 'G-L-E-N-W-O-O-D'. But as they arrived at 'D', the DHS boys would roar out 'D-H-S' followed by 'School! School!' As DHS had the numerical advantage, the roar was deafening.

---

[120] Maties came first. The name was given to them by UCT students because they kept calling each other 'maat' (mate). Later, the Maties nicknamed UCT 'Ikeys' because of the number of Jewish students at the university and a silly bit of verse that started 'Ikey Moses, King of the Jews'.

[121] Durban High School was the second of John Scott's secondary schools. However, Pietermaritzburg were keener on the cost-sharing idea and so Maritzburg College is older than DHS – which was founded two years later in 1865. In contrast, Glenwood was only founded in 1910, didn't move to its present site until 1920 and was not known as Glenwood High School until 1934.

[122] This rivalry is epitomised by a tradition known as 'the ringing of the school bell'. On the Friday evening before the derby, with the excitement of the fixture growing and a fair number of the old boys from both schools lacking in sobriety, a brave venture into the enemy would be made. Then, as midnight approached, some of the younger old boys would venture onto the property of the other school and ring their memorial bell. Unfortunately, schools have entered the days of outsourced security, and this has ended the daring raids.

[123] So bad was the problem at one stage that detention involved catching a bottle full of locusts before being allowed to go home.

But Glenwood has grown steadily since those days. Now, with 1,200 boys enrolled at the school, and with Gibson House having tripled its number of boarders in a matter of years, they can more than hold their own when it comes to pre-match war cries and their performances on the rugby pitch have similarly blossomed, with the Glenwood First XV now appropriately nicknamed the 'Green Machine'.[124] In fact, today Glenwood High School can boast of one of the most professional schoolboy set-ups in the country – with fitness and skills training beginning at seven o'clock every winter morning. They employ specialist coaches for the forwards and backs – as do many schools these days – and there is also a conditioning coach. But you will not find money, bursaries, professionalism or conditioning at the heart of any school's rugby success. You will find *people*. In schools rugby, that means those patient teachers and coaches that plough countless hours into the boys that arrive on the high school treadmill. They are the folk that epitomise rugby and its spirit. At Glenwood one such coach goes by the name of 'Toppy' Hortop.[125]

Old boy John Allan once described Toppy to me as the 'oldest living teenager'. Beginning his 29-year coaching reign at Glenwood in 1970, the English teacher was instrumental in growing interest in rugby at the school, but more significantly, ensuring that the boys played the game in the right spirit – an issue on which he could happily speak to anyone for hours.

His birth certificate says William Anthony Frederick, his wife insists on Anthony, but to those countless pupils, colleagues and acquaintances he has always been and always will be Toppy. A charismatic maverick, Toppy has always done it his way. While this approach hasn't always made for smooth sailing, it has,

194

---

[124] Boarding numbers have risen from about 90-odd less than a decade ago to nearly 300 today.

[125] This section on Toppy Hortop is largely indebted to the words of the coach himself, a speech he delivered at a Glenwood Rugby Dinner (2008) and the reminiscences of his good friend and fellow Glenwood teacher and coach Rob Hutchinson.

to his eternal credit, been interesting, different and sometimes dangerous.

Toppy is recognisable, first and foremost, by his beard, something he has had since his year in the army. Playing for the u20 side, his debut against the Blue Bulls lasted all of five minutes before their lock 'moved' Toppy's nose to beside his right cheekbone. It was about this time in his life that he decided never to shave again, as a protest against all forms of educational, military and political stupidity. In fact, he was the first long-haired, bearded player to run on to Kings Park (it was not Cobous van der Westhuizen as many still assume) – with Reg Sweet, the doyen of Natal rugby writers at the time, describing him as 'hirsute and lacking sartorial elegance'. Which, interestingly, he still regards as a compliment.

However, it wasn't long before Toppy returned to his roots, or rather, to the school that perhaps should have been where his rugby career began.

As a fine young rugby player at St Henry's in the 60s, Toppy had often been encouraged to join Glenwood and play for one of the province's finest rugby school. Eventually he did go but only to attend the Natal Schools' Trials.

Koos Basson, a great bear of a man, said to the young Toppy in his strong Afrikaans accent, 'Hortop, what are you doing here?'[126]

'Sir,' he answered, 'I've come for the trials.'

Koos looked at him with pity and said, 'Hortop, you bloody fool, the trials were yesterday!'

But Toppy couldn't escape Glenwood forever and after finally graduating, he took a job coaching the young grasshoppers (and teaching some English on the side).[127] So it was that upon

---

[126] Koos Basson coached arguably Glenwood's finest rugby side in 1965.

[127] He also coached a number of Natal Schools' sides, both before and after integration. The 1984 side ranked among the best, and included the likes of Joel Stransky, Gary Teichmann and Steve Atherton.

Glenwood's fields Toppy won his admirers, especially in the great rugby schools of College and DHS. And in Glenwood's classroom, his empathy and real concern for his pupils endeared him to them. They felt his commitment and responded in kind (and sometimes with golf balls and bottles of the fiery liquid). However, these days Toppy is saddened by parents who put their sons on the market, looking for the best deal, and the scouts and their blatant attempts to persuade talented youngsters to join their 'academies'.

'For all the denials, no school is guiltless,' Toppy told me. 'Coaches too are on the money trail. The term "loyalty" appears to have lost its meaning and the camaraderie that, in the past, was so much part of the joy of coaching, seems a distant memory. What was highly regarded as essential to a child's development by most teachers, coaches and parents is now regarded as nothing more than an opportunity for short-term personal gain. The days when boys would gratefully inherit a pair of boots from their elder brothers seem part of another era. These days players get sponsored "warm-up kit" and "warm-down kit" and so on. And if they are any good at all, they get invitations to play for other schools. And they go!'

The inevitable changes have not left the coaching staff unaffected either.

'The days of hardy coaches who were either teachers or parents have also gone,' Toppy continued. 'Today, many coaches are highly paid individuals lacking any idea of the point of sport within an educational milieu. To face and appreciate 30 to 40 testosterone-filled youngsters five times a day in the classroom, and then on the sports field, allows one considerable insight into the "making and breaking" of the human spirit.'

The root of much of the problem has been the incoming professional wave. Mammon rules.

'Many years ago, Doc Craven predicted that professionalism would rip the heart and soul out of sport,' Toppy lectured. 'Sadly, in some respects, he was spot on.'

From two rooms, seven pupils and one reference book (a small *Chambers Dictionary*), Durban High School has come a long way. Most notably, it has produced some of the most remarkable men in South African sport.

In 1910 the sport-mad Aubrey Langley, whose nickname was 'Bull' to some and 'Madevu' (moustache) to others, became DHS headmaster and put an end to School's traditional leanings towards the round ball.[128] A disciplinarian first and foremost, he was also a man of contrasts: you didn't know if he was going to give you a good caning or put two shillings in your hand. However, he was School's first rugby coach – bringing his heavy hand and passion for the oval ball from Maritzburg College.[129] And although he was truly 'old school', I am certain many a parent would be only too pleased were Langley to roll out of his grave and lay down his law to the youth of today. Certainly, DHS flourished under his leadership.

The eras of Langley and the great coach Bill Payn overlapped at both Maritzburg College and DHS. An extraordinary schoolmaster and sportsman, Bill Payn coached the First XV from 1932 to 1957 as well as representing Natal at six sports.[130] In 1922 he ran the Comrades Marathon in rugby boots, had a good breakfast at Hillcrest, finished eighth, and then played a Murray Cup fixture for Durban Collegians the following day at fullback in 'tackies'.

Bill Payn served Natal Schools' Rugby, including being

[128] Langley thought small schools (which School was at the time) would never be great schools if they played both rugby and soccer.

[129] While Langley was at Maritzburg College it is said that he was riding upon his horse around the Alexandria Grounds when he noticed two Maritzburg College boys playing with a soccer ball. He prompty got off his horse, opened his penknife, and with a powerful stroke deflated the spherical ball. He disciplined the boys with a caning each for disobeying the 'new soccer laws'.

[130] Having served in France during World War I, Bill Payn also interrupted his coaching at DHS to serve in World War II. Near on 50, he fought with anti-tank guns in North Africa. He received the Military Medal, but not before he was captured and put in a POW camp where he suffered terrible illness.

coach and then chairman for 18 years. In recognition of his contribution to rugby, the 'Old Crocs' trophy was renamed the 'Bill Payn Trophy'.

A DHS coach who had a great influence upon international rugby was Izak van Heerden. After fighting in World War I, he returned to DHS to teach and coach, and soon proved especially successful in the latter.[131] He was largely responsible for the resurgence of Natal rugby and Tommy Bedford once spoke of the coach as 'streets ahead of his time', adding that, 'Natal had no star players in those days. We could not poach talent like Northerns, Transvaal or Western Province, and we had no real executive power to protect our interests, but we did have a genius as the coach.' Later in his career Van Heerden was sent by the South African Board to Argentina, where he trained the Pumas so well that they defeated the Junior Springboks at Ellis Park in 1962. In fact, it is perhaps Argentinean rugby that is most indebted to his work, for he laid the technical foundation for their strong packs (that continue to plague international opposition today). He also penned many acclaimed books and was president, coach and selector of numerous councils and clubs. But throughout he served DHS and it was in his office in the old school hall itself where he died in 1973 – after 39 years on the staff.

Izak often came across as a quiet man – someone who did not have to make a point by raising his voice; it was his sheer physical presence that earned everyone's respect. Tall, with thick-rimmed glasses above a salt-and-pepper moustache, he was known for always wearing a tailored suit and, more often than not, a silk bow tie during his Afrikaans classes. However, as a coach, he was distinctly old school.

As rugby was a compulsory winter sport, Izak led a beginners' class at Berea Park for those who had not played the game in

198

---

131 Taken prisoner in World War I, Izak soon escaped and lived on the run for nine months, often without food and a number of times perilously close to recapture.

primary school. There, he would split the 60-odd new boys into two teams; one team in School colours, the other in white. Then Izak would calmly toss the ball onto the field and settle down to watch the ensuing mayhem, clipboard in hand, ready to record a player's name if he showed some vague talent.

But spare some sympathy for the lad who came from the 'wrong school'. One Lionel Cason once vividly described the punishment dealt out at his first u15 practice of the year. While seated with the other boys on the sidelines of a pitch known as 'The Matchbox', Lionel saw Izak moving swiftly along the line finding out each boy's previous school. He had been warned to avoid mentioning the fact that he had attended Overport Primary School as Mr van Heerden had a certain dislike for some junior schools, but by the time the large coach arrived, Lionel, intent on shoving a piece of grass into his mate's ear, had forgotten his instructions. Caught unawares, he blurted out 'Overport School, sir!' before he could stop himself.

The coach studied him for a second, before shouting, 'That's a bloody soccer-playing school, so run to the end of the field and back!' Then, turning to the rest of the boys, he yelled, 'The rest of you go and kick that bloody fool's arse!'

Lionel immediately set off with about a hundred guys chasing him, all eager to kick him up the arse. However, the 'exercise' may have ultimately worked in Lionel's favour as he enjoyed two years of First XV rugby as a speedy winger.

As the boys soon learnt, this was Izak's favourite party trick and no doubt brought him hours of joy over the years.

Leaving Durban behind me I pushed on up the N3 to Pretoria. I had met many great rugby people in KwaZulu-Natal and enjoyed my time in this historic province, but the second Test was around the corner and Loftus Versfeld beckoned.

FROM KAALVOET
TO THE LIONS

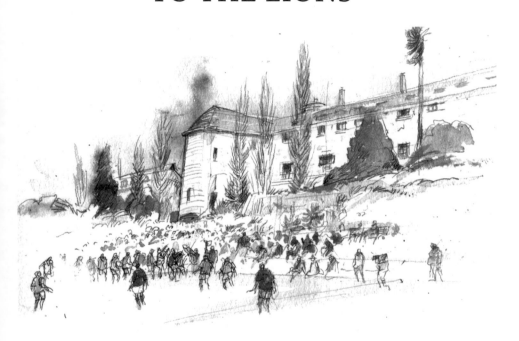

St John's

Late June – Early July 2009

DIE BOERE OORLOG

Even at the height of apartheid the Anglo-Boer War was still being fought in the streets of Sunnyside and its neighbouring suburbs. Needless to say this spirit spilled over onto the sports fields and was particularly evident in the derby between the two finest rugby schools in Pretoria: Afrikaanse Hoër Seunskool, or 'Affies', and Pretoria Boys' High School, or 'Boys' High'. Befittingly dubbed the 'Boere Oorlog', the clash between the two schools was, at the very least, an intense affair, but more often than not an hour of absolute carnage with some rugby in between.[132] However, as political change moved through the country it was finally realised that the Boer War was over, and though supporters on both sides are still zealots, so too are they a remarkably similar breed. This rugby animal, most easily identified when a young man is a new member of the old boy club, seems to adhere to certain rituals and dress codes no matter which side he supports:

---

[132] The link to the Boer War is never far away in these games. A British field hospital and POW camp (where a young British journalist named Winston Churchill was once imprisoned) occupied the stony ground where Boys' High now play their rugby and when the Department of Public Works brought in gangs of convicts to level two pieces of ground and to clear away the stones they exposed a dump of old medicine bottles – which made tackling rather hazardous on certain parts of the field.

Old Boy Checklist:

✓   Collared shirt
✓   Old boy tie, or if this is already lost, a school tie will do
✓   Navy jeans
✓   Oakley sunglasses
✓   A sauntering swagger that goes with this new-found freedom
✓   A hot blonde held closely at your side. (Ignore the 'immature' sniggers of disbelief from the staff and younger members of the school you've left in your wake for far grander things)

Such old boy freshmen are most prominent at the biggest derbies on the calendar, and in Pretoria their vociferous support – for one side or the other – is always readily available.

Will Hofmeyr and Bill Brooks, the last member of staff to play for the school, spent decades at Boys' High coaching the boys and building formidable sides to take on their near rivals, and it wasn't long before the derby with Affies grew so big that it had to move to nearby Loftus Versfeld.[133] More recently, Eddie Dorey took up the coaching mantle.[134] The irony was that he was Afrikaans and when he arrived at the 'Engels' Boys' High, he could barely speak a word of English. He was rather partial to wielding the cane, and according to one Trevor Quirk many a forward received a couple of stripes across the backside if they

---

[133]   Bill Brooks played for Boys' High Second XV vs Harlequins in 1925. Staff playing in school teams was a common occurrence in South Africa at the time. As well as making up the numbers, they offered a much-needed physical presence on the field – especially considering that most rugby games were against men's club sides. Of course, games against other schools were desired, though the likely institutions in nearby Johannesburg were slow in picking up the oval ball. In 1922 *The Pretorian* moaned: 'When shall we be able to covert the four erring sheep in Johannesburg, which, for some super-sensitiveness, only cast hankering glances towards the fold of the national game?' The four erring sheep were KES, Jeppe, St John's and Parktown, schools more inclined to the Association code.

[134]   I am indebted to Deirdre Hickman for the information on Boys' High coaches.

didn't pack low enough or push properly. He was a real man's man, who pretended to rule with a rod of iron but actually had a heart of gold. After school on a Friday, the first team would meet in the sports pavilion for chocolate cakes, 'coolies' and a team talk, during which he threatened to 'bliksem' them if they didn't stick to the game plan.

A prominent name in rugby and especially schools rugby is that of ex-Boys' High coach Paul Anthony. Known as the 'Lion of Lebanon', he coached two of the current Bok hookers – John Smit and 'Chilliboy' Ralepelle – and a number of others who went on to play international rugby for other countries.[135] However, his vocabulary needed to be studied to be understood. A young Chinese boy, who did not play rugby, once complained to another teacher that Paul was a racist. Asked how he came to this conclusion, the boy responded, 'He always says, "Howzit, my china" and does not use my proper name.' Of course, this was his greeting to all and sundry.

Two other Boys' High coaches also require mention.

In 1985 Peter Blauw, an old KES boy, arrived to coach the First XV for a few seasons. He was an ambitious coach, but he was also rather superstitious. One year he was due to depart for Potchefstroom at six am when he realised that he had taken his 'lucky slacks' to the dry cleaners and had forgotten to collect them. Pandemonium! He could not possibly leave without them. The manager of the dry cleaners had to open the shop and after much searching (Peter did not have the receipt with him), the trousers were finally located. Eventually, he left for Potch at half seven. He arrived in time for the game and – hallelujah! – Boys' High won.

In contrast, Loedewyk Potgieter, a rotund music teacher, knew nothing of the game of rugby. But, as with most schools, it is

---

[135] Chilliboy was the first-ever black captain in Springbok rugby. Perhaps, after labelling certain schools fly half and flanker factories we should call Boys' High a 'hooker factory'. Of course, Grey College doesn't count, as they are arrogant enough to produce players in *every* position.

the expectation that teachers at Boys' High participate in some coaching capacity. Loedewyk was put in charge of the 10th rugby team, also known as the 'Boom Span'. Running up and down the sidelines, with his A5 Theory Manuscript book holding all his coaching tips, he would shout all the things he'd overheard 'real' coaches say, although these were rarely used in the right context. At the back of his book he would write down the names of those who scored tries, and later each of them would be rewarded with an ice-cold Coke. Coke sales at Boys' High soared, as did attendances at the 10th team fixtures as the rumours of Potty's eccentric coaching style spread.[136]

Good coaching, however, will always yield good players. John William Smit, born 3 April 1978 in Pietersburg, played in the Boys' High First XV from 1994 to 1996, and was head prefect in 1996. He arrived a tennis player, but finished as a hooker who was destined to go places in the young professional game.

Smit is my kind of a rugby player; a bloke all too aware of the game's old-fashioned values. As a winger, I could never presume to know what happens among the fatties at a scrum, but Smit appears to me to be the epitome of an experienced, shrewd hooker. His size (not lack of skills, I'm certain) has meant that the front row, the part of the field where it is said that brain and brawn collide, would always be his place in rugby.[137] But Smit's craftiness has meant that he has even been able to reinvent himself as a prop, to accommodate that fine hooker, Bismarck du Plessis. This slight shuffle along the front row was also immediately advantageous for Smit himself as an unwritten rugby rule allows a prop to do less work around the pitch than the hooker. But it is his leadership which perhaps separates him from most, something which his current Bok coach was recently

---

[136] Sadly, the much-loved coach passed away at a relatively young age.

[137] Strangely enough, this is often a position held by the brightest in the team. Accountants and doctors have for many years made up the front row in Springbok rugby. Perhaps their work stress in such intensive professions dictates that they must play in the front row to let off some steam.

keen to point out in his own inimitable style: 'John is the greatest leader I have worked with,' De Villiers said. 'He even has the ability to take a wrong decision and to get everybody to believe in that. Then you really are a good leader.'

Just below Waterkloof Kop, and the lush campus of Boys' High, stands the proud stadium that is Loftus Versfeld. Within its shadow is Affies, the cradle of some of the finest talents in world rugby, including Pierre Spies and Fourie du Preez.

Among the thundering Bulls herd, Spies is an athletic specimen with few peers. One of the most physically powerful eighth men in modern rugby, indeed in the game's history, the devoted Christian was cruelly denied a trip to France for the World Cup when he was struck down with severe kidney problems. For Spies, then, this Lions series offers a chance to deal with some unfinished business on a stage all of the rugby world will be glued to.

Fourie du Preez has established himself as the world's finest scrum half. However, his Lions counterpart, Mike Phillips, is also quickly developing into a great scrum half, and it was these match-ups that would be under the microscope at Loftus in the second Test.

THE SECOND LIONS TEST
(27 JUNE 2009)

The Lions tour first arrived in South Africa in 1891 and though it was a squad made up of only English and Scots it swept all aside on its way to:

Played: 20
Won: 20
Points for: 226
Points against: 1

That solitary try belonged to one Charles 'Hasie' Versfeld – guaranteeing him lifelong hero status – but it was Hasie's brother who was immortalised.[138] Loftus Versfeld was named after Robert Owen Loftus Versfeld, the founding father of organised rugby in Pretoria, in 1932. The last time the Lions ventured onto the field at Fortress Loftus, Adrian Richter's Northern Transvaal won 35-30. This time around the administrators had wisely decided that two of the three Tests would be played on the highveld.

The festivities had long been underway at Loftus Versfeld by the time I arrived. Every square foot of grass in a two-kilometre radius of the stadium had been annexed with braais and beefy

---

[138] The suffering faithful would have to wait a few more years before things were to improve. However, by the turn of the century, the days of easy pickings for the British and Irish tourists were gone for good. Having lost just one of 40 matches on their first two visits to South Africa, the home unions representatives would win only half of their 22 contests when they returned in 1903 and lost the est series 1-0 with two internationals drawn.

cooler boxes, and sokkie classics were blaring out over the crowds gathered around the beer tent.

I had never imagined that my Loftus debut would be among those who had no knowledge of the taal, but my ticket had me shuffling through a sea of red Lions jerseys until I found a lone seat between two plump Poms. The crowd was warming up and the repetitive chant of 'Lions! Lions! Lions!' and the melodic 'Oh, I'd rather be a Lion than a Bok ...', sung to the tune of 'She'll be Coming Round the Mountain', filled the air around me.

The Lions needed a win to breathe life into the series and the final Test; the Boks hoped to kill it off. With passions at their zenith, there was always going to be plenty of niggle and physicality. Every time a scuffle took place, I had my Lions beside me screaming '99!' Burger, perhaps a sentimental selection (his return for a 50th cap after an injury lay-off), was the first to fall foul of overzealous behaviour.[139] He eye-gouged in the first minute and the ref responded with a yellow card – something that would later end his chances of playing in the final Test. But despite his foolishness I couldn't help pitying the man who a year earlier had glowed with excitement at the idea of the impending series.

The Lions dominated the first half. The first-Test hero, Beast, was crushed in the scrums by Adam Jones, and Simon Shaw, a tall man among tall men, brought the fire that had been lacking in the first Test to the Lions pack. And on top of it all the Boks missed the kicks.

But influential moments that swung the game in the Boks' favour arrived in the second half. The strong Lions scrum was nullified to uncontested when Jones and Gethin Jenkins departed injured, and men like Brüssouw and Jacques Fourie, who ought to start any Test, also brought late intensity as Pretoria's altitude began to tell on the visiting side. As the clock

209

---

[139] He replaced Heinrich Brüssow, the revelation of the tour.

ran down, with groggy and beaten souls sidelined, Ronan O'Gara stood at fly half, winger Tommy Bowe inside of him and Stephen Jones pushed to the outside centre. With their puff fading, the fatal error was made by O'Gara. Morné Steyn, displaying a calm no player winning only his second cap should be allowed, then sent the 53-metre penalty over as the hooters blared. The game was over and the series secured. With disbelief all around me, I punched the air: victory!

FINAL SCORE:

Springboks	28
British and Irish Lions	25

A WEALTH OF RUGBY

The sprawling city of Johannesburg was not always the destination for the business-minded. Originally, it was an area snubbed by the British, but the Gold Rush of 1886 changed all of that forever. Brit and Boer fought for control of the land, while representatives from much of the known world arrived in the humble mining camp to seek their fortune. The town grew and grew, men arriving in their droves to work in the mines, and where there is a conglomeration of young men in South Africa there is almost always a wealth of rugby.

Upon dusty fields devoid of kikuyu grass the game developed and the Transvaal soon became one of the strongest rugby areas in the land. Fast forward to Basil Kenyon's amateur team that toured Britain in 1951-52, and you can see just how important the mines were to the growth of the sport in this area:

Hennie Muller: compound assistant
Hansie Oelofse: mine surveyor
Johnny Buchler: mine clerk
Basie Vivier: miner[140]
Frans van der Ryst: shift boss
Ben Myburgh: assistant superintendent at a mine hospital
Piet Wessels: journalist
Jan Pickard: wine taster[141]
Gert Dannhauser: bottle-store manager
Okey Geffin: contractor
Des Sinclair: salesman
Buks Marais: 'traveller'
Basie van Wyk, Willem Delport and Chum Osche:
                        schoolmasters
Basil Kenyon: wool broker
Salty du Rand and Ryk van Schoor:
                        tobacco farmers in Rhodesia
Cowboy Saunders: detective[142]

Those were the days – when a rugby player was just another bloke and not a rugby clone produced in a school academy. Wouldn't it be great to look up Bakkies Botha in the Pretoria Yellow Pages under Plumbers for Pretoria or search the Internet for Smit & Beast's Funeral Parlour? At the very least, we could drag them over for a quote and have a yarn about their Saturday game. I'm sure they'd love it.

211

Perhaps because amateurs weren't bound by disciplinary

---

[140] Basie Vivier would later captain the Springboks.

[141] Jan Pickard later became a millionaire from his dealings in the liquor trade and other businesses.

[142] With thanks to Gerhard Burger for the details of the players' professions.

committees and told off for 'bringing the game into disrepute' their personalities seem to have come to the fore and wonderful stories of the 'old days' abound. One such bloke was Tommy Crean, who though a thoroughbred Brit, did not leave Africa without stamping his remarkable influence upon it.

Crean came to South Africa with the 1896 Lions team, an Anglo-Irish combination. Johnny Hammond of England was the captain but Crean was the real leader and at times he led his teammates a merry dance. At the start of the tour the team were invited to Groote Schuur to have lunch with the prime minister of the Cape Colony, Sir Gordon Sprigg, before going on to Newlands to play Western Province. Crean insisted that his team each drink seven glasses of champagne – no more, no less. After their lunch they went off to Newlands and drew 0-0 with Western Province. The teams met again later in the tour and this time the sober Lions won 32-0, still the biggest defeat Western Province has suffered against the tourists.

After the tour Dr Crean of the Royal College of Surgeons settled in Johannesburg and was in practice in the rough mining town. On one occasion he was shaving when a man burst in to ask for medical help. Crean was incensed – he was naked at the time – and said to the man: 'How dare you enter my premises while I am shaving naked? You have an ugly face. I want to fight you.' The man fled with the naked Crean after him, brandishing a shaving brush. Back at his house the man locked Crean outside, but the good doctor refused to leave and stood outside bellowing to him to come out, while a crowd gathered. Eventually, a policeman arrived and gave Crean his jacket to cover his exposed private parts. Wearing the coat like a kilt Crean stalked home in high dudgeon.

Crean was in Johannesburg when the 'South African War' (Anglo-Boer War) broke out. He joined the Imperial Light Horse as a trooper and in 1901, at the Battle of Tyergkloof, he was wounded twice, which enraged him, and crying 'I'm kilt entirely!' he rose up and charged the Boers. He was awarded a Victoria Cross.[143]

He was invalided out of the army in London but at the outbreak of World War I, in spite of the fact that he was married and the father of two children, he again joined up. At the Battle of Mons the British forces suffered heavy losses, including all its medical men except Crean. When his commanding officer saw him walking about, smoking a cigarette and attending to the wounded, he ordered him to take cover, but Crean put an arm around the officer's shoulders and said: 'General, m'darling, 'tis written that I shall die in m'bed. The boys need me. Go I must.' He went on attending the wounded till sunset. This time he was decorated with a DSO.

He died in his bed, as he had predicted, in London on 25 March 1923, aged just 49.

Gauteng (the old Transvaal) is littered with stories of the personalities that graced the amateur game, but what of their legacy? Happily, South African schools rugby in this part of the world is still alive and well. In fact, despite some of the problems it faces, it seems to be getting better by the day, and the growing numbers that attend the derbies and festivals are testimony to this. I'd chosen four schools, each with a unique heritage, to tell the story of the development of rugby in and around Johannesburg.

---

[143] One of four international rugby players so honoured (three of them having played for the Wanderers F. C. Rugby Club in Dublin).

JEPPE

And the first thing that struck me about the place was that nothing had changed in the course of a quarter of a century. That, I felt, was as it ought to be. From the outside, the main building (with the date 1909 above the pillared entrance) looked just like it did when I was a scholar there a quarter of a century before. I was very pleased about that. There had been no attempt at that vain and deceitful thing called 'progress' during the intervening 25 years. I looked at the green shutters that were badly in need of paint. There was something about them that gave me a sense of solid satisfaction. It is right that they don't stick too much green paint on those shutters ... – Herman Charles Bosman[144]

The son of a miner (who died in a mining accident), Bosman finished his schooling at Jeppe, excelling in literature and drama. He eloquently answered his final algebra paper with an essay devoted to explaining why he could dispense with the subject since his English was so good. Like Bosman, most of us despise too much progress at our alma mater, even if it is only greener shutters. Some progress is good. Like more computer rooms and rugby poles. But most of us prefer our school to stay just as we remember it.

Jeppe High School for Boys opened in 1890 with 25 boys between the ages of seven and 13. School fees were set at three guineas a term. Rugby was not much of a sporting option in those early days, largely because of the grass – or lack thereof – and it was soccer, where your face was not planted into thorns

214

---

[144] Extract from *Jeppe High Revisited* (ed. Stephen Gray).

and dirt, and where your long shorts remained relatively clean, that became the dominant code. However, when the boys were finally converted to rugger, they took to it with aplomb.[145]

One talented Jeppe old boy – a Springbok from the 50s – is Wilf Rosenberg. I had arranged to meet with him at his Illovo flat after work (he still works eight to five for a consultancy company). With charcoal hair and alert eyes large behind dark-rimmed reading glasses, the short man in his mid-70s greeted me warmly and led me up the three flights of stairs to his flat that overlooks the Wanderers Cricket Club.

As the son of a wandering rabbi, Wilf is proud of his Jewish heritage and framed photos of his extended family – spread across South Africa and the world – lay scattered around his room, covering every inch of vacant space. 'I came to South Africa from Australia because of my dad's work,' Wilf began, settling upon the edge of his bed. 'I went to Grey High initially, and then up to Potchefstroom – to Boys' High. Unfortunately my father changed his congregation like he changed his underpants, and after the summer terms at Potch I was off to Johannesburg and Jeppe, where I represented that school's first undefeated rugby side.'

It was during these years that Jeppe would produce one of rugby's greatest centre pairings in Wilf and Des Sinclair. They had flair, acceleration and fine movement – ideal attributes for good centres. Initially, though, Wilf's tackling ability was questioned. 'Doc, you've got that tackling machine out at Stellenbosch,' Stephen Fry said to Doc Craven at the Queens Hotel in Cape Town before the second Test against the 1955 Lions at Newlands. 'Can't we bring it here so that Wilf can be taught how to tackle properly?'

'Stephen,' Craven replied, 'you know today is a Friday and

---

[145] Their polished soccer skills weren't wasted. In rugby's early days, dribbling past the opposition (the forwards often used to dribble the rugby ball) was rather common.

the Test is tomorrow, and we never practise on the Friday before a Test.'

But Fry insisted. So the tackling machine duly arrived and Doc put Wilf through his paces. The next day he tackled Davies right out of the game – Butterfield and Davies were at that stage regarded as the best centres in the world.

The Doc had a special appreciation for the young man's talents.

'At 17 years of age I was the youngest player to represent the senior Transvaal rugby team,' Wilf said. 'And from there Danie looked after me.'

'Craven had a superstition that he wanted a Jew in each side,' Wilf laughed, 'but I could never understand his motivational speeches before each game. They were always in Afrikaans, and having spent my formative years in Australia, I didn't understand a thing. Craven told me: "My son, you'd better learn the language quickly." He gave me Karel van Vollenhoven as my roommate. We couldn't communicate. I couldn't speak a word of Afrikaans and he couldn't speak English. But that's why Craven put us together.'

But in 1960 Wilf left for Rugby League – his father having signed him up while he was still on honeymoon – and began a successful stint at the English Club. 'Doc hated players taking a penny from the game,' Wilf reflected. 'When he visited me in Leeds he said, "Wolfie, please don't play professional rugby. Come to Stellenbosch. You'll learn to speak Afrikaans and play for us. But please don't play for money." I was heartsore, but I didn't want a lawsuit against me, and the club had treated me very well.'

A framed photo of that team still hangs upon his wall. He points at a player. 'He was as dirty as hell! That guy punched with a closed fist. League is the roughest, toughest and dirtiest sport in the world!'

In the days of few internationals, Wilf only ever played five

Tests for the Springboks, beginning in 1955. His final game was against France at Newlands in 1958 and, despite League's fierce physicality, it was in Union and this Test where he sustained his worst injury. 'I was smashed by four Frenchmen in a tackle,' he told me. 'I wanted to get up but I couldn't. I looked down and it seemed my foot had disappeared. It was hanging in the opposite direction. Some of the French actually cried! I wasn't exactly rushed to hospital either. An ambulance only picked me up at the after-match function.'

He then began to rattle off a catalogue of horrific injuries, from dislocations, to fractured jaws and broken fibulas. 'I'm no advertisement for rugby,' he chuckled, 'but I still wouldn't change a thing. Rugby's been good to me and given me so much.'

And he's not the only Jeppe old boy to feel like this. Jake White – another of Jeppe's alumni – is arguably South Africa's most influential rugby man in recent years. Holding fiercely to the traditions and values of the Bok jersey, he continues to grow the game and nurture rugby's indispensable grassroots.

ANCHORMAN

Despite many of those on the highveld speaking with an accent that could curdle cold beer, almost all South Africans have come to enjoy the familiar tones of proud Joburger Hugh Bladen. He has been the voice of rugby since he first took to the airwaves in 1976 – the year mainstream television was launched in South

Africa – and was due to commentate on the third Lions Test that Saturday. It would be his 156th.

I had arranged to meet Bladen at his Rivonia complex. Johannesburg seems to be one complex after another, adapting and changing as it has always done, I thought as I waited for the electric gates to open before descending to his house. These days Bladen's time is largely his own, and is divided between work for various trusts and boards, writing and golf. But then he is semi-retired, having spent 35 years in the jewellery trade.

He offered me a Coke (the morning was still young) and lit a cigarette, and we took a seat in his green, shaded backyard.

I get the rugby CV over with first – star sportsman at school; fly half for the Wanderers Club, Transvaal and the Junior Springboks; vice president of the Golden Lions Rugby Union; commentator.

'I had no aspirations to commentate,' he told me. 'It just came about.'

While on the *Castle Lager Sports Quiz* in the mid-70s with some Wanderers teammates, Kim Shippey, manager of SABC Sport and a commentator himself, noticed that Hugh seemed rather comfortable on national television. And as he had a rugby background, he was duly asked to do the deed. His first 'trial' was commentating for the Transvaal v All Blacks game in '76. But things really kicked off a few years later. In 1980, the British Lions arrived, and as Trevor Quirk and Shippey were in England (covering Wimbledon) Bladen was drafted in as cover. He 'called' his first game in the third Test in PE and the rest is history.

In the early days Bladen told me that he and Chick Henderson used to joke that it 'cost them money' to commentate – the 25 rand they were paid a game barely covered their travel costs – but all that changed with the advent of professionalism and the growth of SuperSport. In 1995 Russell Macmillan, then of M-Net, urged Bladen to commit himself to M-Net in return for a monthly fee. However, SABC Sport had asked him to cover the '95 World Cup, to which they had sole rights. 'Blades' asked Macmillan if he could join after the World Cup. The response was – 'You come now or never!'

A brief call to Louis Luyt resolved the issue. 'I think this company is going to buy rights to all rugby in South Africa,' Luyt wisely warned Bladen.

Blades signed up, in the process losing out on the chance to commentate on the '95 World Cup, but gaining the chance to anchor on SuperSport, the channel that would soon have the monopoly on rugby in the country.

Bladen is always the anchor; the one who calls the game. His sidekick is the comments guy; the likes of Joel Stransky, Toks van der Linde and Bob Skinstad – ex-players who may be able to offer some additional insight. They sit together in the commentary box – the quality of which varies dramatically. Twickenham's box, at the '99 World Cup, was no better than literally sitting in a stand of commentators, all beside each other, shoulder to shoulder. Occasionally, the arrangement is rather more open-plan, as in France 2007. But on that occasion, during the tense quarter-final, an excitable Argentinean commentator got so wound up in the action that he hoofed Blades in the back.

The director sits outside of the stadium in a broadcasting van that resembles 'the cockpit of a Boeing'. From there, he directs the cameramen, the commentators in the box and on the sidelines and numerous other things. Even as Blades introduces the television audience to the players there is a constant *voice* (no, not God, but the director) in his earphones.

'And I thought multitasking was for the ladies!'

'Ja,' Blades laughed, 'I've asked my wife why she can't talk on the phone and to me at the same time.'

Bladen's pre-game prep is some research in his annuals and books. From there, useful information is filtered into the secretary's notebook from which he commentates: names, numbers, stats and history. On the day, it will translate into a bit of a school oral – the painful prep is done, the flip cards are prepared, and you hope it all comes together at the time.

There are a few things to be avoided when commentating. Perhaps the most obvious is 'not knowing your wingers from your props', though this can be hard not to make a mess of when you're due to commentate on a Samoa-Georgia game at the 2003 World Cup. Consider this horrific Samoan name:

Sailosil Tagicakibau

Now say it again, this time as it should be pronounced: an 'n' before the 'g' (as in Tana Umaga = Tana UmaNga) and the 'c' becomes a 'ch'.

Or how about the Georgian winger and fullback:

Malkhaz Urjukashvili

Badri Khekelashvili

The last name is especially difficult for the soutie – the 'k' becomes an Afrikaans 'ge'.

'By the time I got the names right,' Blades said, 'they'd taken the conversion and were kicking off again!'

To his credit, Bladen has never taken himself too seriously, though it would seem that this is a change from his days at King Edward VII School, where he reckoned himself a rather 'intense' student. Hugh told me a story to illustrate his point. After narrowly scraping a victory in an u13A away game at Parktown his fiery Scottish coach had been furious at the 12-year-old Hugh and his teammates. 'Go home!' he told them.

Hugh took his words to heart, turned and began to trudge wearily home – from Parktown back to distant KES in Houghton! – the rest of his team trailing in his wake.

My own experience of KES is linked inextricably with the colour red. The buildings are red – the brick looking as fresh as it did nearly a century ago – and the First XV, too, play in red.[146]

Initially, as was the norm in Johannesburg, the school played

---

[146] In 1982 the original part of the Houghton building was declared a national monument.

soccer, but when grass was finally laid, KES turned to rugby (in 1931) and has been one of the strongest schools in the country, year in and year out – as befits a boys-only school with strong boarding credentials. Each year it fields over 20 teams.

KES has the proudest sporting record of the English-speaking schools in Johannesburg and quite possibly north of the Vaal River. If it has any sporting rivals among the other English-medium schools within a 100-mile radius it is one of the three other 'Milner' Schools: Jeppe, Pretoria Boys' High and Potchefstroom Boys' High.[147]

There is also good reason for both KES and St John's being in St Patrick's Road in Houghton. Initially, the two were more than just rivals upon the sports field ...

ST JOHN'S

St John's is without a doubt one of the most magnificent schools in the country.[148] Red-tiled stone buildings gaze out from a ridge which drops dramatically down to the rugby field.

The Reverend John Darragh is regarded as the founder. He

---

[147] Although state-sponsored, these schools were consciously modelled on English public schools by the then British High Commissioner for South Africa, Alfred Milner. Built after the end of the Anglo-Boer War, in 1902, they were part of a move designed to help Anglicise the Transvaal and eradicate Afrikaner culture and the Afrikaans language.

[148] This section is much indebted to the work of Richard Mayer (St John's 1980-84).

persuaded his parish council to open an Anglican school for boys.[149] But the school they raised the money to build did not immediately develop into one of the country's most exclusive schools.[150] British High Commissioner for South Africa Alfred Milner opposed the very existence of private schools, and under his leadership the Transvaal administration actively sought to force the closure of St John's, by not only establishing a powerful rival in the KES but also by attempting to draw scholars away from St John's and into the ranks of its rival. With the College battling to attract scholars in the difficult period after the war, the government actually went so far as to send a circular to the parents of St John's boys pointing out the advantages of sending their sons to the new state school. *Venture of Faith*, the official school history of St John's, characterises the new school prospectus which St John's issued in response as the work of a 'somewhat desperate David [throwing down] the gauntlet to the governmental Goliath ...'

When the government educational authorities decided in 1907 to relocate KES to a site a mere 150 metres away from St John's, officials and supporters were left with the unavoidable impression that the utmost was being done to crush the fledging church school. The Reverend James Nash, the celebrated headmaster of the school at the time and a member of an order of Anglican monks who had saved St John's during its precarious early beginnings, felt the threat strongly.[151] After his retirement as headmaster, his gift to the College was a reproduction of

---

[149] Darragh had already been the founding force behind St Mary's Anglican Girls' School in Waverley, the oldest school in Johannesburg, and he would give impetus to the founding of the school which would eventually grow into the King Edward VII School (KES).

[150] The parish raised 800 pounds for the school and promised support in the amount of 300 pounds per annum. John Darragh's curate, the Reverend J. L. Hodgson, became the first headmaster.

[151] He stated his deep misgivings regarding the motivations behind the choice of a site for KES and stated, 'I fear it may alter our hitherto friendly relations with [KES]. It will be much if we can keep the peace.'

Verrocchio's 'David' from the Bargello Museum in Florence. It is also no coincidence that when the statute of David was installed in 1934, in what became known as the David Quadrangle on the eastern side of the College, it faced in an easterly direction – towards KES![152]

Rugby at St John's started in 1934. Two things were needed for the birth: a grassed playing field and a good deal of instruction regarding the rules.

A dusty expanse below the amphitheatre, bounded by Valley Road, was where the grass was grown.[153] Today it is where home games are played and where the St John's Easter Rugby Festival takes place.

Instruction in the rules of the game was the task of Jack Huggett, the Afrikaans teacher. In the old wooden Alston House and on the edge of the hill that overlooked Major Yates' shooting range, Mr Huggett set about explaining on his blackboard that the principal rule of rugby was the backward pass, a foreign concept to the gathered boys. It seemed to many confused souls that gaining ground was going to be quite difficult. The overlap as a means of scoring was also greatly emphasised by the patient coach, though many boys struggled to understand how that advantage could be achieved. However, it wasn't long before the boys got the hang of the game and soon a more than healthy rivalry was developed with KES.[154] The terraces were always crowded, both schools in full attendance, and many came without affiliation to either but only a healthy interest in the finest schools rugby.

223

---

[152] But despite such inauspicious beginnings and an early history of bitter rivalry, KES has always been regarded with admiration and respect by the older St John's boys. Sport and in particular rugby was the main point of contact between the two schools and the boys.

[153] Prior to the grass being sown the stony field was used as a venue for punishments: any misdemeanour and one was sentenced to an hour after school of picking up pebbles.

[154] The annual game used to be known as the Charity Match.

A wise coach with infectious enthusiasm can be one of the most influential figures in a young man's life. Recently, St John's have had a fine coach in Norman MacFarland (who coached at KES before that). But one Maxie Burger is also a legendary figure at the school and the main field has recently been named in his memory. A plaque at the field reads: *In affectionate memory of Willem 'Maxie' Burger, inspiring coach, teacher and administrator for 31 years.*

Maxie's appointment was fairly unusual at the time as there were very few Afrikaans-speaking teachers on the staff, but he quickly endeared himself to boys and teachers alike. He used to smoke untipped cigarettes, which meant that most of his instructions were interspersed with a *thp* as he got rid of little bits of tobacco from the end of his tongue. One of his instructions went like this: '*Thp thp*, now I want the ball to go from the scrum half, *thp*, to the fly half, *thp thp*, then to the centres and the wing, *thp*, and the loose forwards must be there, *thp*, to fall on it.' Ultimately there would be a loose mielie left on the field.

He even came up with a way of using the school's 'Englishness' to its advantage on the rugby field. Being an expensive, boys-only private school, St John's had the inevitable reputation of being elitist among its rivals. It was also – according to many government-schoolboy cynics – filled with 'poofters'. Because of this it was often said that someone in the St John's pack would say, 'More pressure in the rear, St John's!' as the packs got down to business. Maxie decided to use the 'fact' to St John's advantage in a game against Jeppe. During the game, both scrums readied themselves for the put-in, which was about five yards from the Jeppe line. Jimmy McPherson, a fine hooker, leaned back between his props and said in the plumiest of voices, 'Oh come on, St John's, more pressure in the rear!' The Jeppe scrum packed up laughing; that was until St John's wheeled the scrum and scored. Then, I suppose, it was not quite so amusing.

Rugby is all about enjoyment, especially when your side is

losing. One of rugby's finest sons and ambassadors, Morné du Plessis, once visited St John's in 1982 to remind the boys of the game's values. He had recently retired from international rugby, and after some stirring words in the morning, he taught some of the boys the finer rugby arts in the afternoon. To illustrate a particular skill he asked one Stephen Fasulakis to run against a line of players passing the ball from one end to the other. The point was to prove that the ball would always beat the man, and thus should always be passed. However, for the first time in Du Plessis' experience, the man beat the ball. 'This guy must be pretty fast!' he exclaimed with some surprise. Fasulakis went on to beat the school 100-metres record with a 10.8 later that year.

In every South African all-boys school (especially those with a large boarding contingent) rugby deeply permeates the very fabric of school life. At St John's, rugby is compulsory and all new boys – gingerly know as 'Removes' – are dragooned into playing the game unless they can prove they are medically unfit.[155] Tradition like this keeps unity and identity. Daily prayers in the chapel; processions of servers, incense and a therifer;[156] the roll call response of 'Ad sum' (I am present) each day – fine traditions and fine rugby. Brilliant!

---

[155] The term derives from the English public school system and signifies that the boy has *moved* from the preparatory school to the senior school.

[156] Since opening with 11 boys, the sons of congregation members, St John's has remained true to its spiritual roots. It has produced more Anglican clergy than any other school.

SAINTS AND FESTIVALS

The game was against the old Afrikaans rival and neighbour Randburg Hoërskool. For 1998 St Stithians head boy, captain of rugby and eighth man Jock Seeliger this was a game which St Stithians had to win. School and rugby pride was at stake, and Saints were narrowly leading when the ref declared the final movement of the match. Jock looked decidedly panicky as the packs readied themselves for the final put-in, and he aggressively encouraged his exhausted forwards into one final effort. Scrum half Rory Montgomery fed the scrum, possession was kept and the ball neatly presented back to the scrum half. Rory gathered and proceeded to clear the ball over the touchline to win the game for St Stithians. He held his hands aloft, enjoying the sweet sound of the final whistle. But only for a moment. Jock, in an incensed rage, turned to his scrum half and screamed in his face, 'What the hell do you think you are doing? It was the last movement and you have cost us the game!'

Rory stood rather bemused, the rest of the team looking on in wonderment, as Jock hailed down a barrage of curses upon his scrum half. Rory managed to calm his captain down, and point him towards the scoreboard one more time. It read of a three-point victory to St Stithians. Gathering himself, Jock, in a decidedly relaxed fashion, patted Rory on the back, 'Oh, I thought they were leading. Sorry. Well done!'

The game and ensuing entertainment took place on Saints's main rugby field, the Baytopp Field. It is really a miracle that this field is as fine as it is today. In its early days it suffered from poor drainage, but groundsman Len Baytopp put his back into laying a new field in the early 70s. And true to boys'-

school tradition, boys were required to assist in reseeding the field. However, a few bored Saints 'labourers', who shall remain nameless, thought it a good idea to toss a few mielie seeds in with the grass seeds in retaliation. Consequently, Mr Baytopp witnessed a rather unique rugby field develop, one that would keep him especially busy that season.

But despite the school's relatively short history, its Baytopp field can boast of having set a precedent that these days can be felt in almost every corner of South Africa. It was, after all, on this field that the first rugby festival was held. Though Craven Week and Cape Schools Week were in existence, in the early 1980s no one school hosted an annual festival designed to draw together teams from schools across the country. St Stithians began theirs in 1983, during the Easter holiday, and numerous other schools have subsequently taken up the idea. The Easter rugby festivals are popular and allow schools to compare their team's strength with the others on show and gauge how competitive their season may be. More importantly, however, they are good for establishing and renewing relations between schools. Competing teams share downtime with their erstwhile rivals: they eat, practice and train together. But the real beauty of these festivals is that there is no man of the match or tournament hero, nor is there a trophy or reward to be won.[157] As such, festivals can offer scintillating, running rugby between schools that are usually unable to play one another due to distance constraints.

The festivals do, however, serve to boost a school's own rugby prestige, and Johannesburg has traditionally had a monopoly on hosting these festivals. This seems to be changing, and a number of new festivals, for a variety of age groups, have mushroomed across the land.

Many of South Africa's schools have special ties because their histories overlap. The two Greys – College in Bloemfontein and

---

[157] Though they are, increasingly, events where many of the national and international rugby scouts can be spotted.

High School in Port Elizabeth – share a *founder* and thus a big derby. Other schools are drawn to one another because of their denominational ties, such as the Anglican heritage shared by Bishops and St Andrew's. The Methodist schools of St Stithians and Kearsney play each other regularly, and it was Kingswood, the Methodist school of Grahamstown, that first gave rise to St Stithians.

The Saints festival has hosted the finest rugby schools in South Africa, and some of the greatest Boks of the last twenty-five years. The pioneers instrumental in getting the festival going were Tim Clifford and Colin Hall. Clifford was in charge of rugby from 1972-86, and was a fanatical, eccentric Irish coach. His team talks – a blend of blarney, passion and patriotism – were legendary, and he would regularly invoke Ireland and her saints to motivate his young charges.

Half of the fun of a rugby tour is the travel – perhaps even more so if you're on your way to Grey in Bloem and you know that only a solid thumping awaits you – and Tim Clifford loved to tour by train, especially to Cape Town and Port Elizabeth. The train travel was very cheap in those days and schools got a handsome discount – the boys paid ¼ fare. On one such memorable tour, Pixie Louw, a burly 18-year-old lad, couldn't sleep. Although he wasn't about to admit that he was a Bryanston softie, the bed felt harder and harder as the train stopped at station after station. At one such stop, Pixie saw a stack of railway mattresses on the platform. A gift from God and ripe for the taking! Moments later he had a mattress once more. But it stank to high heaven – of urine, vomit and stale beer. From an open window of the now speeding train, the mattress was sent like a Scud missile into the dark abyss.

Unbeknown to Pixie, however, the radar-eyed conductor had spotted the errant projectile as he scurried past the windows of the dining saloon and he soon raised the alarm. Coaches Henny Jansen and Tim Clifford were poring over a chessboard, brandy glasses on a table beside them, when the little conductor with his peaked cap disturbed them. A practised look of horror spread across his face as he took in the two masters, who were manifestly oblivious to the coup breaking out in the compartment two doors away. One could envisage the banner headlines on the front page of the *Sunday Times*:

Gotcha! Posh Boys' School on Railway Rampage!
The Masters Play Chess while Rome Burns!

Henny, sensing an outburst from the crazed Irishman, intervened smoothly in Afrikaans. Profuse apologies and a bottle of brandy did the trick. The conductor would not put them off the train nor would he report the incident to the police – provided they paid in full for a new mattress.

Next morning, at a team meeting in the dining car, Pixie Lowe offered an explanation: 'Sir, it was meant to be a temporary expropriation, but the dear mattress didn't meet even the minimum health or hygiene standards and therefore I gave it a merciful and speedy end.'

He certainly had the gift of the gab, but though the masters were sure it was just a schoolboy prank, action was required. Clifford held the whole team responsible – they would have to pay for a new mattress and a bottle of brandy. 'And you, Pixie Lowe,' he said, 'collect the cash and bring it to me.'

A couple minutes later Pixie knocked on the door of the coach's coupé. Hale and hearty, he said, 'As first-team coach, sir, you have the honour of making the first contribution.'[158]

229

---

[158] Unfortunately, Pixie Lowe met with a tragic end. Three months after the events in this story took place, he was dead: impaled on the handlebars of his motorbike (a machine he had built himself over three years). As his coffin was being brought from church to the hearse, the first team formed a guard of honour to bid a last farewell to their teammate. It was the saddest day of Clifford's coaching life, indeed of his teaching life.

THE THIRD LIONS TEST
(4 JULY 2009)

A final Test against the Lions remained. It would be held in Johannesburg at Coca-Cola Park – the new sacrilegious name for the historic Ellis Park. Lions tours must be confusing outings for the tourists, who were certain their previous games in South Africa or New Zealand were held in grand old stadiums with names like Kings Park, Lancaster Park, Athletic Park, Eden Park (and Ellis Park). I suppose for a million rand players might consider changing their own names; a rugby pseudonym if you like: Sasol Habana, Vodacom Bakkies or Tiger Wheel & Tyre du Plessis.

Even with a series won, there was a lot riding on this game, especially for the Lions. It was a chance to show that they still had pride in the jersey, and to end on a high a tour that had re-established the old Lions traditions – players roomed together, mixed with supporters, took time to visit townships and orphanages. So it was that on the pitch the Lions dealt out the rugby lessons, displaying 'total rugby' to a Bok team not hearty or shrewd on the day.

The game swiftly edged away from the Boks and only the final whistle put an end to their misery, but spirits were lifted as the series trophy was raised aloft by Smit. As international rugby spectacles went, this tour had been memorable. The Lions may have yet to win a Test series in the twenty-first century, but this is a fine tour and a tradition that has reaffirmed its importance and put faith back in the red jersey.

They'll have to wait until 2021 to have another crack at the Boks; for now, the Lions circus moves to Australia.

FINAL SCORE:

Springboks	9
British and Irish Lions	28

AMEN

While 'the Battle of Waterloo may have been won on the playing fields of Eton', the success of the Springboks is much indebted to the fine rugby schools scattered across these old lands.[159] I'd been to some of the finest nurseries of rugby talent in the country and met some of their great players and coaches, in the process discovering that the pure form of the game, which continues to breed our finest youngsters, remains well fed and watered.

Arriving back at my flat in Cape Town, where my rugby crusade had begun a year and a half earlier, I took stock. The pockets felt somewhat emptier, but I counted myself fortunate to have been able to visit some of the greatest rugby stadiums in the world and to have met some of the wisest men in South African rugby.

My journey had ended where it had first begun: upon the fields of the Diocesan College. And I knew that, between the white lines where the great game was played out, the stories would emanate and later be retold around braais, each tale growing taller by the year.

---

[159] According to an old Etonian, the Duke of Wellington (the Honourable Arthur Wellesley while at school).

GLOSSARY

Alma mater   Used of the school, college or university from which you have graduated. Fancy Latin words that literally mean 'nurturing mother', though the former sounds far more manly.

Amadoda   A respectful word for 'men' in some African languages. Not to be confused with bafana.

Braai   Staple diet in South Africa. Involves men standing around for hours speaking little sense while liquids are consumed and meat is cooked over an open fire. Usually concluded with a rugby game.

Barbeque   English version of a braai, though only done once or twice a year. The red meat in this case is burger patties.

Diaspora   South Africans fleeing crime, the rand and BEE.

Dop   An alcoholic beverage.

Dorp   Afrikaans for small country town – where most of the Bok rugby talent is bred.

Haka   All Blacks' pre-match jig – clapping of thighs, eye-balling, tongue-stretching, et cetera. The Poms would have the haka banned, but South Africans don't really care because we haven't bothered to translate it and so are happy for the additional entertainment.

'Howzit, my china?' Hello.

Klap   To forcibly exert pressure via an open hand or closed fist upon an unwitting opponent. A rugby klap is best done when your opponent is at the bottom of a ruck and has no clear view of you. For a legal klap, see tackle.

Roasties   Grass burns that are proof (to the girl you are courting) that you do, in fact, play rugby.

Saffa   South African in London, apparently working legally but quite possibly otherwise.

Soutie   An 'Englishman' in South Africa. Having one foot in England, the other in Africa and his manhood dangling in the Atlantic.

'that other version' Rugby League (only mentioned in hushed corridors and followed by 10 Hail Marys).

'the others'   Rugby League players. Gained notoriety in the TV series *Lost*.

Train lag   Very similar to the jet lag experienced by the Springboks, only worse. At its worst after a Saffa has endured lengthy travel on London's Underground to reach work or home or a rugby pitch.

Poppies   Young Afrikaans girls. At schools rugby games they are also commonly referred to as groupies.

Ruck   Free-for-all. Sometimes a rugby ball is involved. The referee prefers it if you enter the pile-up from your own side.

Tackle 'Wrapping two arms around your opponent's waist with your head resting on his bottom' (as I was taught by my coach). This definition varies around the rugby world. In Fiji, for instance, an opponent is legitimately tackled around his neck, whereas in Scotland the term rarely has much use these days.

Matthew Knight was educated at Selborne College and has studied Theology, History, Literature and Education. He is the co-author of *Derby Day: South African Schoolboy Rugby* that featured the history and rugby of over 100 schools. He harbours ambitions of one day donning the Springbok green and scoring a try against the All Blacks, although he wishes to first establish himself as a vital cog in the Guy's Hospital Vets XV.